Meeting Customer Needs

Third edition

Ian Smith

chartered
management
institute

ELSEVIER
BUTTERWORTH
HEINEMANN

AMSTERDAM BOSTON HEIDELBERG LONDON NEW YORK OXFORD
PARIS SAN DIEGO SAN FRANCISCO SINGAPORE SYDNEY TOKYO

Elsevier Butterworth-Heinemann
Linacre House, Jordan Hill, Oxford OX2 8DP
30 Corporate Drive, Burlington, MA 01803

First published 1994
Reprinted 1994 1995
Second edition 1997
Reprinted 1998, 2001, 2002
Third edition 2003
Reprinted 2004

British Library Cataloguing in Publication Data
A catalogue record for this book is available from the British Library

ISBN 0 7506 5948 X

Typeset by Keyword Typesetting Services Ltd, Wallington, Surrey
Printed and bound in Great Britain by Biddles Ltd, King's Lynn, Norfolk

For information on all Butterworth-Heinemann publications
visit our website at www.bh.com

Contents

Series adviser's preface

This book is one of a series designed for people wanting to develop their capabilities as managers. You might think that there isn't anything very new in that. In one way you would be right. The fact that very many people want to learn to become better managers is not new, and for many years a wide range of approaches to such learning and development has been available. These have included courses leading to formal qualifications, organizationally-based management development programmes and a whole variety of self-study materials. A copious literature, extending from academic textbooks to sometimes idiosyncratic prescriptions from successful managers and consultants, has existed to aid – or perhaps confuse – the potential seeker after managerial truth and enlightenment.

So what is new about this series? In fact, a great deal – marking in some ways a revolution in our thinking both about the art of managing and also the process of developing managers.

Where did it all begin? Like most revolutions, although there may be a single, identifiable act that precipitated the uprising, the roots of discontent are many and long-established. The debate about the performance of British managers, the way managers are educated and trained, and the extent to which shortcomings in both these areas have contributed to our economic decline, has been running for several decades.

Until recently, this debate had been marked by periods of frenetic activity – stimulated by some report or enquiry and perhaps ending in some new initiatives or policy changes – followed by relatively long periods of comparative calm. But the underlying causes for concern persisted. Basically, the majority of managers in the UK appeared to have little or no training for their role, certainly far less than their counterparts in our major competitor nations. And there was concern about the nature, style and appropriateness of the management education and training that was available.

- British managers are undertrained by comparison with their counterparts internationally.
- The majority of employers invest far too little in training and developing their managers.
- Many employers find it difficult to specify with any degree of detail just what it was that they required successful managers to be able to do.

Under the umbrella of the National Forum for Management Education and Development (NFMED) a series of employer-led working parties tackled the problem of defining what it was that managers should be able to do, and how this differed for people at different levels in their organizations; how this satisfactory ability to perform might be verified; and how an appropriate structure of management qualifications could be put in place. This work drew upon the methods used to specify vocational standards in industry and commerce, and led to the development and introduction of competence-based management standards and qualifications. In this context, competence is defined as the ability to perform the activities within an occupation or function to the standards expected in employment.

The series was originally commissioned to support the Chartered Management Institute's Diploma and Executive Diploma qualifications, which were one of the first to be based on the vocational standards. However, these books are equally appropriate to any university, college or indeed company course leading to a certificate in management or diploma in management studies.

The standards were specified through an extensive process of consultation with a large number of managers in organizations of many different types and sizes. They are therefore employment-based and employer-supported. And they fill the gap that Mangham and Silver identified – now we do have a language to describe what it is employers want their managers to be able to do – at least in part.

If you are engaged in any form of management development leading to a certificate or diploma qualification conforming to the national management standards, then you are probably already familiar with most of the key ideas on which the standards are based. To achieve their key purpose, which is defined as achieving the organization's objectives and continuously improving its performance, managers need to perform four key roles: managing operations, managing finance, managing people and managing information. Each of these key roles has a sub-structure of units and elements, each with associated performance and assessment criteria.

The reason for the qualification 'in part' is that organizations are different, and jobs within them are different. Thus the generic management standards probably do not cover all the management competencies that you may need to possess in your job. There are almost certainly additional things, specific to your own situation in your own organization, that you need to be able to do. The standards are necessary, but almost certainly not sufficient. Only you, in discussion with your boss, will be able to decide what other capabilities you need to possess. But the standards are a place to start, a basis on which to build. Once you have demonstrated your proficiency against the standards, it will stand you in good stead as you progress through your organization, or change jobs.

So how do the standards change the process by which you develop yourself as a manager? They change the process of development, or of gaining a management qualification, quite a lot. It is no longer a question of acquiring information and facts, perhaps by being 'taught' in some classroom environment, and then being tested to see what you can recall. It involves demonstrating, in a quite specific way, that you can do certain things to a particular standard of performance. And because of this, it puts a much greater onus on you to manage your own development, to decide how you can demonstrate any particular competence, what evidence you need to present, and how you can collect it. Of course, there will always be people to advise and guide you in this, if you need help.

But there is another dimension, and it is to this that this series of books is addressed. While the standards stress ability to perform, they do not ignore the traditional knowledge base that has been associated with management studies. Rather, they set this in a different context. The standards are supported by 'underpinning knowledge and understanding' which has three components:

- Purpose and context, which is knowledge and understanding of the manager's objectives, and of the relevant organizational and environmental influences, opportunities and values.
- Principles and methods, which is knowledge and understanding of the theories, models, principles, methods and techniques that provide the basis of competent managerial performance.

■ Data, which is knowledge and understanding of specific facts likely to be important to meeting the standards.

Possession of the relevant knowledge and understanding underpinning the standards is needed to support competent managerial performance as specified in the standards. It also has an important role in supporting the transferability of management capabilities. It helps to ensure that you have done more than learned 'the way we do things around here' in your own organization. It indicates a recognition of the wider things which underpin competence, and that you will be able to change jobs or organizations and still be able to perform effectively.

These books cover the knowledge and understanding underpinning the management standards, most specifically in the category of principles and methods. But their coverage is not limited to the minimum required by the standards, and extends in both depth and breadth in many areas. The authors have tried to approach these underlying principles and methods in a practical way. They use many short cases and examples which we hope will demonstrate how, in practice, the principles and methods, and knowledge of purpose and context plus data, support the ability to perform as required by the management standards. In particular we hope that this type of presentation will enable you to identify and learn from similar examples in your own managerial work.

You will already have noticed that one consequence of this focus on the standards is that the traditional 'functional' packages of knowledge and theory do not appear. The standard textbook titles such as 'quantitative methods', 'production management', 'organizational behaviour', etc. disappear. Instead, principles and methods have been collected together in clusters that more closely match the key roles within the standards. You will also find a small degree of overlap in some of the volumes, because some principles and methods support several of the individual units within the standards. We hope you will find this useful reinforcement.

There is still some debate about the way competencies are defined, and whether those in the standards are the most appropriate on which to base assessment of managerial performance. There are other models of management competencies than those in the standards. We should also be careful not to see the standards as set in stone. They determine what today's managers need to be able to do. As the arena in which managers operate changes, then so will the standards. The lesson for all of us as managers is that we need to go on learning and developing, acquiring new skills or refining existing ones. Obtaining your certificate or diploma is like passing a milepost, not crossing the finishing line.

All the changes and developments of recent years have brought management qualifications, and the processes by which they are gained, much closer to your job as a manager. We hope these books support this process by providing bridges between your own experience and the underlying principles and methods which will help you to demonstrate your competence. Already, there is a lot of evidence that managers enjoy the challenge of demonstrating competence, and find immediate benefits in their jobs from the programmes based on these new-style qualifications. We hope you do too. Good luck in your career development.

From 2nd Edition
Paul Jervis

Introduction

What has changed since the last edition? It's not just the tools and technology that have improved – your competitors are better than they were before and customers know more and expect more than they ever have. The most important lesson? Those who sit back and try to rest on their laurels will be left behind.

EVERY BOOK NEEDS A MISSION STATEMENT

The strangest thing about this book is that we should need it at all; but we do. Nobody manufactures products simply because it is a nice thing to do and services that no one needs survive only in history books or in fiction. Products and services have no purpose without customers and yet here we are considering the idea of meeting customer needs as if we didn't do this all day and every day we work.

We could explain this by showing that there are customers within organizations as well as being served by organizations. This book addresses internal markets and is here to help the reader identify and meet customer needs across the whole of their working lives. Lack of understanding of internal customers is not the only reason why a book like this is needed.

Sadly, we regularly encounter people and organizations who are failing to meet their customers' needs. Some of these organizations appear to pride themselves on having good relations with their customers. Some believe that they do enough or do not think it's relevant to them. Some even blame their customers for their organization's failings or troubles!

The truth of the matter is we spend the majority of our time at work serving a wide range of customers without analysing what we are doing in a customer-focused way. Our perspective is distorted. We are missing opportunities, losing competitive edge and performing below our best simply because we are not serving our customers well. That is why this book is needed.

The mission statement for this book is as follows:

> *Through sound concepts, practices and experience this book will help every reader to identify, listen to and understand their customers and develop an approach and a set of practices which will help them meet all of their needs, exceed their customers' expectations and win their continued commitment while ensuring a secure, efficient and profitable future for the reader's organization.*

Our mission statement commits us to deliver some very important things but it is also a form of contract, which is entered into by the author and the readers. If the book fulfils its mission statement the reader should have happier customers and a more effective, secure and profitable organization. It is a contract we hope you will be happy to agree to.

WHAT HAS CHANGED SINCE THE LAST EDITION?

The world has changed somewhat since the last edition of this book. A mere five years have seen enormous changes in the world of communications with the explosion and implosion of internet companies, the wild fluctuations in the stock market, 11 September and its aftermath, second- and third-generation mobile phones (and the consequent development of the 'prehensile thumb'), continued globalisation accompanied by the decline of mass markets and mass media, and the permanent appearance of grey hairs on the author's head.

Customers (remembering to include ourselves in this) have become more sophisticated and have a greater choice in a much wider range of products and services. Greater segmentation has led to more complex markets and our understanding of internal and external markets has grown, too.

So, once we have overcome our surprise that this book is really needed it becomes obvious that a new edition is also needed to cope with the changes that have taken place.

HOW DIFFERENT IS THIS BOOK?

This is a completely revised and rewritten book designed to cope with today's problems and issues. It focuses on what we know and understand about customers based on research and consultancy work and it aims to show how we can meet customer needs within the wide range of circumstances likely to be encountered by the reader. We provide the concepts, tools and guidance and you do the rest. It is for managers everywhere and is a practical resource to help you maximize your effectiveness through greatly improved relations with your internal and external customers. Those studying the IM Certificate and Diploma and management courses up to NVQ level 5 will find this useful as will those managers who just want to have a long-lasting and mutually rewarding relationship with all of their customers.

HOW CAN YOU USE THIS BOOK?

There are three strands to this book.

The book can be read from cover to cover and used to help you learn about customers and about how to manage the process of understanding and meeting customer needs whether they are found within or outside your organization. The book covers a wide range of relevant theories, concepts, practices and techniques. Various examples and short cases are used to illustrate these.

Alongside the text lies a series of action boxes designed to help the reader compile their own action file or workbook. This can be put together either on a computer (using appropriate word-processing software) or by keeping a notebook. Either way, the results will give a comprehensive analysis of your own organization, department, job and customers, and a set of actions and strategies to help you become a successful, customer-facing manager well prepared to meet the demands of your work and the assessment at IM Certificate/ Diploma levels and for your NVQ in management.

Finally, there are self-assessment competency questions at the end of each chapter. These are designed to support your learning while preparing you for competency assessment. Use them to check that you have understood and addressed the key points in the chapter.

First, know yourself

Even those who think they know everything about their organization and what it produces or provides need to revisit, review and re-examine. Before they can improve, change or stay on track they need to know themselves. What does the organization produce/provide, what is the path to customers, who are the players involved in the process, how does their department fit into the process, what is success and how is it measured, who are the competitors, and so on?

Starting a new job, even one in a department or organization you have been working for some time, teaches you that you have a lot to learn about both the job and the organization or department. The new position and the perspective it provides usually changes the familiar. You soon see that the role is defined as much by the context as it is by the functions you are required to perform.

Changing into someone who is 'customer facing' can be like taking on a new job. Helping a department to do this may change it into a new department. Imagine what it can do to a whole company!

This chapter covers some of the fundamentals. To meet customer needs you will certainly have to develop a much greater understanding of your customers. You will also have to gain a greater insight into how you and your organization do and see things.

The simple message here is:

> *To meet customer needs you do not change your customers; you have to change yourself!*

So as you learn about your customers you must also strive to learn more about yourself.

CUSTOMERS? WHO ARE THEY?

There are a number of ways of looking at customers but here is a simple outline we can use to describe what a customer is.

A customer is an individual or group of individuals to whom you supply one or more products or services. You may receive goods or services in return or be paid or compensated for this provision through a third party who may also be your customer. These exchanges happen in a number of ways and can form a series of links in a chain which joins with other chains and drives not only organizations but industries and economies.

In purely economic terms each transaction must contain sufficient benefits to each party for the exchange to take place and be sustainable. It needs to be at a price which is acceptable to the customer and which provides you, the supplier, with sufficient rewards (or profits) to induce you to continue with the enterprise. In the non-profit, or voluntary sectors, and in other sectors such as public services and internal markets, profit may not be definable in monetary terms. However, there must still be a satisfactory balance of benefits for both parties.

This will be explored further in following chapters, but you should also consider the following here:

You are a customer inside your organization – As the definition suggests, you are a customer within your own organization. You receive goods and services from other departments and individuals and these transactions form part of the internal customer chain. You need to consider how good your experience as a customer is. Is the exchange a fair one and, if it is not, who is paying the higher price and why? What does your experience as an internal customer tell you about how you serve your own internal customers and what can you learn that will help you when you think of external customers?

You are a customer of (possibly) your own and (certainly) other organizations – Being a customer of your own organization will depend on what it does, but we are all customers of other organizations. It is likely that we will be a customer for everything we consume, use, wear, watch and hear every day. Now is the time to begin to use that accumulated knowledge and experience. If you have never really considered your life as a consumer relevant to how you serve your customers, now is the time to start thinking. Rather than trying to put yourself in the position of the customer, consider this: you are the customer.

ACTION BOX 1.1

Under the heading 'My organization' draw two columns. Give the first column the title 'Customers' and the second, 'What they get'. Now try to list the different customers and what they get from your organization. Try the same exercise with the heading 'My department' and then with 'My position'. Make a note of every customer that appears in more than one list. What do they get out of each relationship and what do you think that means?

YOU ARE A STAKEHOLDER

Part of the balancing process you will face as a manager is being able to meet customer needs while ensuring that the other interests and objectives of the organization are also being met. Part of that balance will be to consider how your actions affect the interests of the organization's stakeholders. Stakeholders include all those with a vested interest in the organization. So, if your organization has shareholders, they would be regarded as stakeholders. However, there is usually a wide range of stakeholders with different interests involved in any organization and most of them have little or no direct financial investment in it. These could include people who hope to be able to use your organization's services one day, those who benefit from your organization's location in a particular town or neighbourhood and

ACTION BOX 1.2

Who has a vested interest in the success of your organization and what can they expect to benefit from this? Make two columns and head them 'Stakeholders' and 'Benefits gained'. Make your list as broad-based as possible. Now go through the list and identify and highlight those who have a direct influence in the organization, those who have some indirect influence and those with no apparent influence.

As a last exercise draw a line beneath the list and put a new heading in the stakeholder column, titled 'Negative stakeholders'. How many people or groups can you identify as having a vested interest in the failure or demise of your organization? Competitors are the obvious ones to list but can you think of any others? Write down what they would gain.

so on. Naturally, an organization's employees may have a vested interest in its continued success, regardless of share or any other form of ownership in it.

BARRIERS TO UNDERSTANDING YOUR CUSTOMERS

Figure 1.1 shows some of the common barriers between you and your customers.

You			
Believe you are doing enough for customers	Lack of contact with customers	Not aware of own attitude to customers	Not fully aware of own role/ position
Your organization			
Departmental ring-fencing	Reluctance to change	Poor communications	Poor/no information — Poor/no research
Situational factors			
Distance from customers	Ignorance of customers	Poor knowledge of customer needs/attitudes	Non-customer view of products/services
Customer barriers			
Customers' ignorance of product/service — Market noise — Competitor activity	Low-level importance to customers	Historical factors	Personal preferences
The Customer			

Figure 1.1
Common barriers between you and your (external) customers.

You will note that there are issues relating to you, your department and colleagues, your organization as a whole, the environment you operate in and the way in which communications work (or fail), and the issues and problems facing your customers. Read this carefully and consider how the barriers you face may not be those faced by your colleagues. Part of your success as a manager is in how good you are at appreciating not only your own problems but also those of your staff and colleagues. In the remainder of this chapter we will explore some of the issues relating to these barriers and help you begin to understand what you need to address in order to manage the process of meeting your customer needs.

ACTION BOX 1.3

Put together your own set of barriers but leave space at the bottom – you may want to add to this list even as you cross out earlier ones.

HOW ORGANIZATIONS RELATE TO CUSTOMERS

The list in Figure 1.1 above illustrates that the type of organization and what it provides helps to determine how it might relate to its customers. For example, companies selling goods directly to other companies will have a different relationship to its customers than a household products' manufacturer in a mass market.

Customer-facing organizations are unlikely to be perfect. Their customers may not be 100 percent satisfied with what they are getting but the organization will be aware of this and determined to listen to their customers, and will continually try to improve things. An organization with very poor levels of customer satisfaction is on seriously dangerous ground and if this is coupled with a general conviction within the organization that they are doing well and do not need to do better it is either an arrogant monopoly or an organization on the edge of failure.

Consider Figure 1.2. Where does your organization lie within the matrix? Unlike most diagrams of this sort, the optimum position is not in the top right-hand corner but at the point marked 'X'. Think about the implications of being in the top right-hand corner. Is the only way down? Of course not! Life is not restricted to a box and you must challenge yourself and your colleagues to find ways of continuing to improve while revisiting your measures of customer satisfaction. Are you so convinced of your perfection that you are forcing your customers to say they are very satisfied even when they are not? How relevant is *your* measure in the eyes of *the customer*?

Now consider Figure 1.3. We will look at this in more detail later, but it is clear from this matrix that we need to please and surprise those customers we wish to win over and fully justify those customers already committed to our products or services. There is no room for complacency in a customer-facing organization.

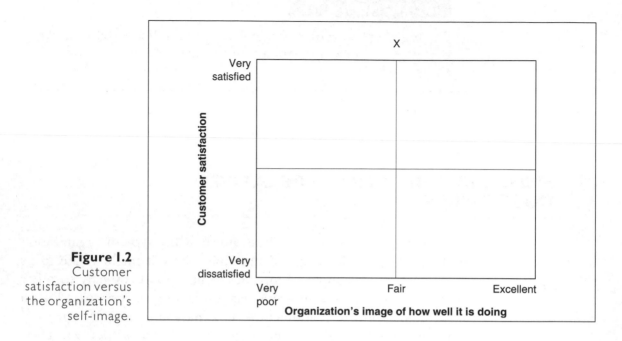

Figure 1.2
Customer
satisfaction versus
the organization's
self-image.

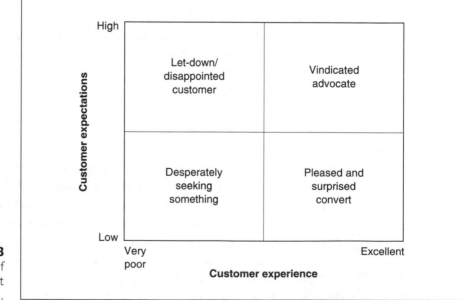

Figure 1.3
The effects of
experience against
expectation.

ACTION BOX 1.4

Write down your honest assessment of how well your organization is satisfying its customers and what would be the most significant improvement it could make. Now select the top three customers you and your department serve. How well are they served and what would improve their experience of you and your department?

ROUTES TO THE CUSTOMER

The issues we need to address when we are trying to improve our relationship with customers are also shaped by the route our products or services take to reach the customer. This is not simply what we in marketing call the 'supply chain'. From your perspective as a manager seeking to develop ways of meeting customer needs within your organization, it is important to be able to position yourself along the internal route as well as within the whole supply chain. While some readers will find it easy to place themselves within the classical model others will be working in roles within large organizations where they will feel that they are completely divorced from external customers.

Let us start by positioning our organizations within the classical model of the supply chain. By using Figure 1.4 to do this we can see how close our organization is to the end-user or customer. One of the typical issues facing companies is how close the company is to the customer and how much control you can have on the relationship with the customer if the supply chain is very long.

The strategies for communicating and developing relationships with customers differ according to your position along this chain, and you may find that you will be competing with companies from one or more of the other 'links' for the same customer. A classic example of this is found in retail. A person who buys a TV from a department store will be regarded as their customer by both the store and the TV manufacturer. In some ways both are correct. The retailer will try to retain the purchaser as a regular customer of the store while the manufacturer will try to retain the purchaser as a customer across the company's range of products. It is inevitable that the two will find themselves in competition over the same customer.

Once you have decided how your supply chain is structured and placed your organization within it, you can look at how you and your

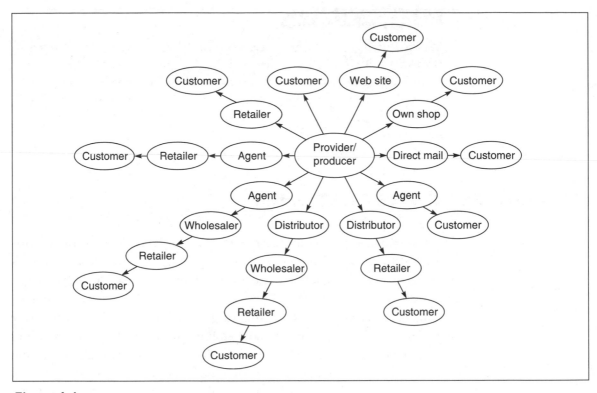

Figure 1.4
The supply chain.

department fit into the picture. What we are most interested in here is how close you are to your organization's customers.

Figure 1.5 is designed to help you think of how your organization will contain a range of functions and departments with varying degrees of involvement with external customers. It also begins to show us how those with no direct links to customers still need to be

ACTION BOX 1.5

On a blank sheet write 'Me' in the centre of the page and 'My organization's customers' at the bottom. Above 'Me' record all of the departments and other organizations that help you in your role. Either side of 'Me' place those who share similar functions or levels of function and below 'Me' those organizations, departments and people who serve the customers more directly than you do or who are between you and the customer. You may have to try this a few times as you think of others to add or change positions until you feel it satisfactorily represents your situation.

customer facing. Each organization is different and this is simply a guide to help you see where you lie within the whole picture.

Figure 1.6 illustrates how you can map your position. You can also do this for other people and departments within the organization and begin to see how your plans will affect those in other departments as well as how directly you will influence the customer's experience of your organization.

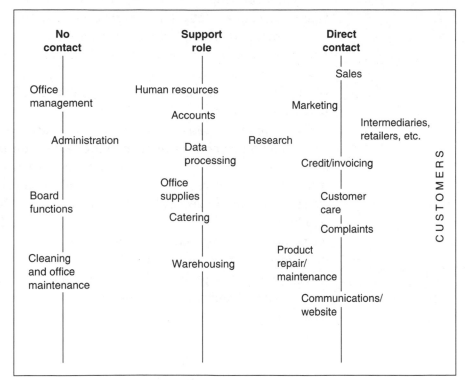

Figure 1.5
Mapping degree of customer contact.

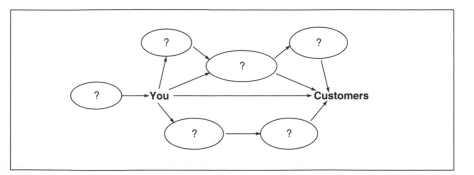

Figure 1.6
Example of a route to customer diagram.

CUSTOMER INTERFACES

Figure 1.5 gives us a picture of the points where customers come into contact with the organization. These are called customer interfaces. We can use these to help us understand more about our relationship with customers by looking at what sort of interfaces they are and why they are there.

Some organizations have a very limited number of interfaces or will only have direct contact if there is a problem. This was very common for manufacturing companies who sold their products through a range of retail outlets. They discovered that the only time they had communication directly with customers was when their products were faulty or damaged. This restricted their customers to only negative opportunities to interact with the company. Hence the introduction of direct marketing and customer-care communications programmes by such companies.

Other organizations are in regular contact with their customers. The dilemmas faced by them may be more complex but the issues are still the same. They include the need to make each customer interaction a positive one, promote the best image of the organization every time, minimize problems and deal with those that occur as quickly and effectively as possible and ensure that at the end of each interaction the customer leaves feeling that their needs have been properly met (even exceeded).

You can gain a great deal of insight into your customer's experience of the organization by looking at each interface and asking the following:

- What happens at this point?
- How does the exchange take place (face to face, by phone, etc.)?
- Who initiates it; the customer or the organization?
- How often does it happen?
- How positive an experience is this for the customer?
- What is its importance compared to the other interfaces?
- What is the value or cost of this to the customer?
- What will its outcome be? (more sales, unhappy customer, etc?)

As with any relationship, the quality of the relationship between customer and company is not determined simply by the number of interfaces or their nature but in how they come together. For example, a specialist service such as a design company may have only one or two people who interface with a given customer or client but those in contact with the client will handle a very wide range of situations ranging from the most complex to the most mundane and from very positive to very negative. How does this differ from a retail bank which provides each of its customers with the opportunity to have a similarly wide range of exchanges, too? How does this compare with buying a new car or doing the weekly shopping?

The customer interfaces help us understand a great deal more about what our customers experience as well as the importance we place on our customers and how we treat them.

ACTION BOX 1.6

Choose one of your organization's customer interfaces that you know well or can find out about and try to answer the questions listed above. Then try the same exercise but with you as the interface and relating the questions to one of your key internal customers. What are the major similarities and differences?

COMMUNICATIONS

Communications are not always two-way. Customers learn about your organization, its services/products and so on through a number of communications channels.

Before any contact has been made customers will learn from your advertising and marketing activities, or from public relations when your organization and its products or services are discussed in the media. Customers also learn from friends and associates and from indirect experience through competitors, etc.

After becoming customers they will continue to learn from those sources while gaining insights and experience through direct contact. Figure 1.3 earlier touched on how important this issue is. Customer satisfaction is directly related to expectations as well as experience so a balance must be struck in your communications so that you never promise things you cannot fulfil while making your offer as attractive as you possibly can. A good example of how this dilemma can be turned into a powerful marketing message was the early Avis campaign where they claimed that they were not the biggest or best. Avis said they knew they were not the top company so they always tried harder. This proved to be a very popular campaign with people believing that Avis were honest in their approach and so could be trusted to try harder than their competitors.

Until recently, advertising, point-of-sale materials and PR were the main ways in which organizations ensured that their current and potential customers were kept informed about their products or services. Direct marketing could also be used to target key markets and provide additional impact as well as disseminate more information to customers. With the advent of the Internet it is now essential for most organizations to produce and maintain a decent website and to make it both easy to find and easy to use. Although, in reality, a broadcast communications medium, the Web gives every individual the opportunity to select and view as they choose. This makes it highly targeted when you ensure that those interested in what you have to offer can find your site and use it easily.

As you look at how your organization chooses to communicate with its customers and what it chooses to say you will begin to gain a greater understanding of both your organization's attitude to its customers and also the experiences and attitudes of its customers.

ACTION BOX 1.7

Draw up three columns headed 'Communications', 'Internal' and 'External'. List all of the communications used within and by your organization and indicate whether you think they are used internally or externally to the organization. How many are actually in use in both contexts? How many do you and your department make use of and which ones should you start using?

INFORMATION SOURCES

At this point the reader will have discovered that the process of meeting customer needs will require information as well as understanding. You will continue to seek information as you work through this book and try to match both your department and your organization to the models and processes covered here.

One of the important sources of information you will use is the range of communications used by your organization. You can access this just as easily as any of your customers and this perspective is clearly important.

Similar information from competitors will also be extremely useful and we will explore how to gather and interpret these data later in the book.

A number of departments within your organization may be able to provide you with other types of information but they *must* all be collected and used only after the appropriate permission has been given. Sources will include the sales and marketing departments, the research department if separate from these, accounts, customer services and so on. The plan for the whole organization may not be available to you but certain parts may be accessible either through the corporate web site or the annual report and through specific managers or directors.

Research reports may not be available but summaries of them might be, and specific information such as customer details might be available from sales and marketing while the research providing the background remains confidential.

Most importantly, the type and range of research on customers that exists within your organization will tell you useful things about your organization. How do you react to the knowledge that there is no research into your customers? What if the research is very superficial? What if it is extremely complicated and detailed? Finding out the answers to 'Why?' and 'What does that mean?' will help you greatly to further your quest.

Finally, colleagues, fellow managers and your line manager or director will prove to be extremely valuable sources of information.

ACTION BOX 1.8

Start a directory in your workbook or diary of all of your current and potential sources of information. Every time you encounter a new source make a note of it here and refer to the directory whenever you are considering new activities, plans or reviews. Also, if you do not already do so, start some files to record all key data on your internal and external customers.

COMPETITORS

If you are serious about wanting to know yourself, your organization and your customers, you will need to learn a bit more about your competitors. How you compare with your competitors provides you with valuable information about how well you are doing, what your potential might be and where some of your threats lie.

The market you are in will determine the ways in which you should compare your organization with its competitors. The most common are value of total sales, volume of sales, number of customers, turn-over of customers, advertising spend, customer profile (types of customers enjoyed by each organization), location of activity and so on.

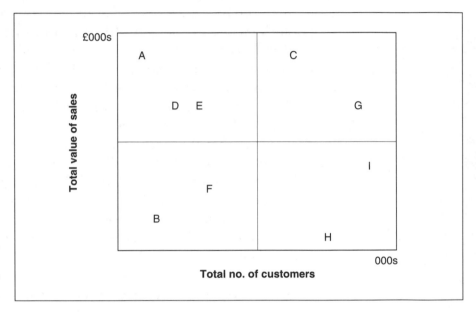

Figure 1.7
Mapping the relative position of competitors.

As with so many aspects of this subject it is useful to explore the information you have in simple visual ways. For example, Figure 1.7 compares a number of companies competing in the same market. The nature of their products and their value are similar. We could use graphs to compare the total sales and the total number of customers but if you plot them together in this way it is possible to see differences at a glance and to argue different strategies within the context of your competitors.

ACTION BOX 1.9

List all of the different ways by which you can measure your organization against its competitors. How many of them are related to customers?

PLAYERS IN THE GAME

The people involved in making your organization run and meet its objectives affect the relationships with customers in a wide range of ways. We have already looked at the routes to customers and customer interfaces; how do the players within your organization influence things?

Here are some ideas to help you rethink how this process can work.

Using the ideas already explored it is possible to divide an organization into the four major groups shown in Figure 1.8 below.

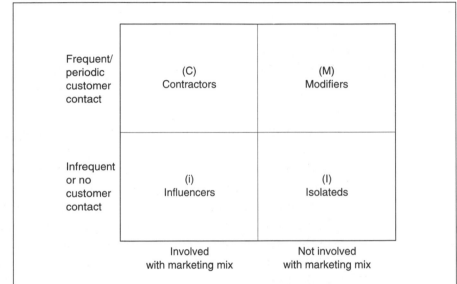

Figure 1.8
Customer involvement with an organization.

Summary
C – Involved in selling, marketing, customer service, and so on.
M – Reception, credit department, switchboard, etc.
i – Research, development, market research, shipping, and so on.
I – Purchasing, finance, human resources, data processing, other support with no customer contact.

From the summary it becomes obvious that the value of communications within an organization cannot be underestimated. Those who prove to be so effective at communicating with the customers outside the organization need to focus some of that talent on ensuring that their fellow employees appreciate the importance and view of the customers the organization needs to serve effectively.

As part of that process of communication and as a tool for learning we can find other sets of roles where the 'Isolateds' in Figure 1.8 are also customers. Using the buying process as our starting point, here are some of the major players involved in buying within an organization:

Roles	Descriptions
Users	Initiate purchase, buy and use.
Influencers	Influence, provide information, evaluate alternatives, may be technicians.
Deciders	Have power to decide.
Approvers	Authorize the proposed decisions.
Buyers	Have formal authority to buy, select vendors, be involved in negotiations.
Gatekeepers	People between sellers and buying department, may be receptionists, secretaries, etc.

Figure 1.9
Roles of people in the buying process.

Source: Wester, W. and Wind, Y. (1972) *Organisational Buyer Behaviour*, Prentice-Hall.

We will use the way in which buying and selling are two parts of the same process to help us develop our plans and strategies later in the book but here we need to begin the process of looking at our organization in fresh ways to help us see how processes affect each other.

One simple example of this is the dual role of the gatekeepers in Figure 1.9. These people may be expected to handle enquiries from both external sales people and the organization's customers (especially in the context of complaints). What can we expect to happen and why?

ACTION BOX 1.10

Place each department in your organization or your division into the four quadrants defined in Figure 1.8. Where did you place you and your department? Write down just one change or addition for each quadrant that would improve the customer awareness of the members in that quadrant.

PLANS, OBJECTIVES AND OTHER GOOD INTENTIONS

In this survey of self-examination we have explored a number of different ways in which your organization might respond to customer needs. The plans, aims and objectives of both your department and the organization as a whole will help you see where meeting customer needs fits in with the rest of its activities. There are a few things to look at carefully here.

First, how much of the plans you have access to deal with customers and with serving their needs? Can you separate the objectives into two sets and how do they balance? How many objectives mention customers, etc?

Second, how many of the objectives can best be met through improving relationships with and servicing of customers? You may find the customers in the detail rather than in the objectives themselves.

Third, how many recognize the process of serving and meeting the needs of internal customers. Does the organization recognize and seek to live up to the idea of being customer facing and does it extend that vision into all of its activities?

ACTION BOX 1.11

Create two columns; one headed 'My organization', the other headed 'My department'. Then write the aims and objectives for each in their appropriate column. How closely are they linked? How customer focused are they?

THE SPOTLIGHT IS ON *YOU*

Despite the chapter's title, the last place the spotlight seems to shine on is you. However, everything so far helps to shine a light on how you fit into the process of meeting customer needs. We expect you to know what your role and position are but we want you to keep re-examining and reviewing what you know in the light of what you learn about customers.

So now you have a better picture of how your organization relates to its customers and where you fit within this big picture. You also have the basis for understanding who your internal customers are and how serving them well will affect the whole process of meeting customer needs. You are compiling the file that will help you maintain excellent customer relations across the board enable you to identify where the problems and opportunities lie when trying to improve customer service and communications.

Finally, the sources of information and the data you have gathered will build on your position as a manager as well as a customer-facing member of the organization. So, what do you expect from the process? Is it enough to believe that by meeting your customer needs you will become a better manager? Of course not.

The process is really the other way round. By becoming a better manager you will meet your customer needs. We are using the focus on customer needs to develop a new and more effective perspective while adding a range of useful and relevant tools to your management skill set. However, the philosophy behind meeting customer needs is important and does make a difference, too. Improvements in this area will increase your competitive edge, improve your effectiveness as a manager and will make the environment you and your colleagues work in more enjoyable and attractive.

ACTION BOX 1.12

Write down two things you can start doing that you believe will make an immediate difference to the quality of service you are giving to your customers. Try to predict what effects these changes will bring about. Start to record any differences you can detect as a result of your changes and plan to monitor the effects over a reasonable period of time (say three months).

Competence self-assessment

1 Obtain an organizational structure chart for your organization and mark on it the level of direct contact each department and player has with the organization's customers. Write down what sort of improvements you might expect to see in customer relations if just three departments or individuals selected by you had some or greater contact with customers.
2 Using the information from this chapter identify the number of departments devoted to serve wholly internal customers and those dedicated to serving external ones. For each department identified, what proportion of their contact with their customers is spent on positive and how much on negative activities (negative being dealing with complaints, solving problems or disputes, etc.)?

3 Name three of your organization's major groups of stakeholders. What key benefits do they seek from your organization?

4 Chose one major stakeholder group with financial interests in your organization and two with non-financial interests. Are they shared with other organizations? How might improved relations with them improve your organization's competitive position?

5 Using your department's current plan, list the aims and objectives directly linked to or shared with the organization's corporate or overall plan. Explain how the remaining aims and objectives do eventually meet the needs of the organization.

6 Try to estimate the proportion of your time spent serving the needs of each of your customers. Construct a table comparing rough averages for you and your department (or the section you are responsible for) as a whole. Rank them from most to least time. Are the most important ones the ones you spend most time on? Explain why.

7 Name two barriers to understanding or listening to internal customers and two more for external customers. Try to choose ones that you believe are out of your control or power to change. What can you do to improve and change things?

8 If you only had two measures to help you evaluate how well you were serving internal and external customers, what would they be? How would they help?

CHAPTER 2

Customers: who do they think they are?

How do we define our customers and how do they identify themselves? If we know what they are like, how they feel and think and what they want out of the relationship we might be able to serve them better! Expectations and experience are keys to satisfying needs. What do customers think and experience and why? What does it mean? How can we find out, examine the problems, look at the barriers and explore these to develop lasting improvements? We must also apply this approach to internal markets.

CUSTOMERS – WHAT ARE THEY LIKE?

Introduction

There was a time when people knew all of their customers personally. Our market place was very local and small then, but mass production and the population explosion changed everything. Now, some types of organization know all of their customers or clients but others have to make sense of the huge numbers of people who buy or utilize their products or services.

Internal markets are usually the reverse of this situation with most departments or individuals dealing with a limited number of people they know well.

Whatever the situation there are a number of ways of helping you understand what your customers are like and define who they are. You can describe them using a variety of characteristics that will help you recognize them and construct a better picture of who you are serving. Although there are an almost infinite number of ways to do this we will explore only the basic approaches and help you find the best ones for your different situations and types of customer.

> ### ACTION BOX 2.1
>
> How many customers do you and your department have? How much time do you devote to them? Count the number of customers you have within your organization and external to it and then make a rough estimate of the percentage of time and resources spent on internal versus external customers. Are there a small handful of individuals or groups of customers who take up a disproportionately large amount of your time or resources? Make a note of these, too, along with your estimates of their share of your own and your department's time and resources.

PSYCHOLOGY OF THE CUSTOMER

Before looking at the ways in which we do the defining and describing, it is advisable to consider the nature of what being a customer is.

We have already defined what a customer is by saying, in effect, it is anyone who buys or receives goods or services from you and may give, in payment, some financial or other exchange. Once we have established that they are indeed our customers, it is advisable to have some understanding of the motivations and thought processes behind their actions.

Culture

Cultural influences can affect buying behaviour in a number of ways. In the UK, we have a number of regional and racial cultural variations which influence purchase decisions. These influences can be very subtle, and many studies have been carried out to try to understand the role of culture. Within each cultural group there are smaller groups each with their own distinctive values. Qualitative research, which is discussed later, is used extensively by marketers who wish to understand cultural issues.

Psychographics

As Philip Kotler points out, 'Lifestyle attempts to profile a person's way of being and acting in the world'. There are two main approaches to lifestyle classification. One uses a long questionnaire broken down into four main topics:

1　Activities such as hobbies, clubs and entertainment.
2　Interests such as home, food and fashion.
3　Opinions on such topics as politics, education and economics.
4　Basic demographic information on each respondent.

The responses are analysed to identify clusters of people with similar lifestyles. When combined with demographic data and analysed against purchasing data, these lifestyle groups can provide valuable insight into consumer motivations. The research company BMRB has carried out a great deal of work in this area using lifestyle questionnaires which have been attached to their large consumer survey, Target Group Index.

The second type of lifestyle classification, developed in the USA by Arnold Mitchell of SRI International, is based on the same technique, but approaches the classification from a psychological point of view. Mitchell explored the values of the individuals in each group and identified nine development stages that people appeared to go through. Each stage affected the person's attitudes, behaviour and psychological needs:

- Need-driven stage.
  - Survivors or sustainers.
- Inner- or outer-directed stage.
  - I-am-me, experientials and societally conscious (inner).
  - Belongers, emulators and achievers stages (outer).
- Integrated stage (achieved by only a small percentage).

In the UK, the market research companies such as Taylor Nelson have developed and successfully used similar classification systems. These systems are interesting, but require a massive amount of initial research work. Their importance lies in their recognition of the value of each individual's personal interests and motivations. They are now used frequently in conjunction with lifestyle databases mentioned later in this chapter.

Psychology

Adam Maslow identified a hierarchy of needs (see Figure 2.1) which suggests that needs are felt at different levels by everyone:

- Basic physiological need for survival.
- Need for protection and security.
- Social needs such as love, belonging.
- Esteem needs such as status or self-esteem.
- Self-actualization needs which involve self-development.

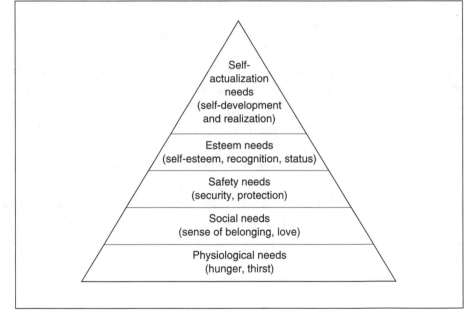

Figure 2.1
Maslow's hierarchy of needs.

Marketers use this and similar models to help them to understand what motivates customers to buy particular products/services. They also use them to design marketing and advertising approaches that harness or awaken specific levels of needs to add psychological support to their advertising messages.

BUYER BEHAVIOUR

Buyer behaviour is the study of how people go about the process of buying, what influences them, what patterns of behaviour do they adopt, how they vary across the population and from product to product or service to service. When considering who your customers are you will also need to ask yourself what your customer's buyer behaviour might be. Without research you will never be certain, but with some idea of what forces may be at work and with your willingness to spend time with customers, observing and talking with them (if you can), you will be able to build some basic ideas in this area.

Here are some issues to consider in relation to buyer behaviour before we look at different types of customer groups.

Buying in a domestic situation

The way in which individuals and families make their purchasing decisions has changed enormously in the last 20 years. Changes include the following:

Individual buying power – Individuals within households have much greater buying power than they ever had. The era of single-income households has gone, children have more pocket money, and there is a wider range of part-time job opportunities than ever before. So many purchases once restricted to family buying excursions (clothes shopping, eating out, etc.) are now being done by individuals within the household.

Decision making – Major buying decisions were once made by one or both adults. Holidays, cars, electrical items and much of the weekly grocery shopping decisions were the preserve of the parents. The pattern today reflects a society where children and young people have a much greater say in what they consume and enjoy.

Product and service range – Choice has expanded as purchasing decisions have become more individual, as markets have become more global and technology has allowed for cheaper, more varied produce and services.

Financial changes – The 'great unbanked' has become a minority, the enormous expansion of credit card availability along with easier loans and other financial facilities have helped to expand the range and buying power of the purchasing population. In 2002, 51% of the UK population preferred to use credit cards to cash when making purchases and 59% said that credit cards were more convenient than cash. Not surprisingly, in the first nine months of 2002 over £91 billion was spent using credit cards in the UK.

Education and aspirations – The population's knowledge of what is possible and available and what they can and should expect has changed vastly in the last 20 years. This has been matched by the population's expectations. So, as we learn more about what is possible, we expect more.

Media and communications – The rapidly expanding range of media available to us was originally described as the fragmentation of mass media. It was reflected not only in the multiplicity of TV channels being made available to us, but also in the larger number and range of radio stations, the expansion of specialist press and the development of video, CDs and DVDs. The explosion in size, range and accessibility of the Web has added to the scale of things, delivering information, entertainment, communications and consumer choice on a greater and more varied scale than ever before.

Alongside the research we do to find out more about our customers we have a broader understanding which helps us ask the right questions and helps us to understand how to communicate and develop relationships with them. Knowing more about who they are helps us predict their likely patterns of behaviour.

Buying in a business situation

Buyer behaviour in the business context can be quite complicated. As you will see later in this chapter, there is often a much wider range of people able to influence the purchasing patterns of an organization and this is one of the reasons why it has been less well studied until recently. The style of management, the structures of authority and responsibility, and the nature and value of the goods or services being bought help shape the size and composition of the group involved in buying. Figure 1.9 in Chapter 1 illustrates some of the roles of people involved in the buying process. All of these groups may require some form of customer strategy in order to maximize your business-to-business strategy. It may be the case that the organization, not the individual, is the customer you are trying to sell to directly. It may also be necessary to win over an individual in order to enable that person to sell your organization to the key people in their company – a sort of reverse internal marketing.

Buying in the internal market

Internal markets may not contain much in the way of competition for your services, but a number of things come into play which mirror what we regard as customer and buyer behaviour in other spheres of business. These include:

Cooperation – The reward one department may enjoy as a result of successful service provision to another department. Cooperation can make things easier to do, quicker to complete and help ensure that the results are of a better quality than would otherwise be expected.

Reputation – The good reputation won by a department through the quality of its delivery of services will provide it with advantages over other departments. Quicker service from other departments, secured budgets, higher status, a stronger bargaining position when required and added leeway or support when things go wrong.

Attitudes – Better internal customer relations result in improved attitudes both towards your staff and shown by your staff, thus helping to ensure continued satisfaction on both sides. Better attitudes towards your department help enhance the other points in this list.

Adding value – Success with internal customers ensures that your department can expect, and will receive, better service from other departments, thus adding value to the department's performance and output. It also enhances the environment and experience enjoyed by your staff, adding value to their working conditions while adding to their personal reputations and standing.

Winning staff – Departments enjoying the benefits described above find it easier to attract and keep good and satisfied staff. This adds to morale and self-image and ensures the continued high performance expected from your department.

ACTION BOX 2.2

In the process of your working day you and your department might serve domestic and business customers as well as internal ones. Divide a page into three columns headed 'Customer details', 'Motivations', 'How I/we recognize and respond to these motivations' (the third column heading can be abbreviated). Then, in the first column, start with domestic customers or customer groups. What do you know or understand about their motivations? Try to identify and summarize them, then consider how they appear to you and your department and how you try to meet or respond to them. If you do not meet them or do so unsatisfactorily highlight or write in colour what needs to be done. Do this for your business and internal customers, too. You should have been aware of much of this but may not have expressed or thought of it in a structured way before.

Rewards – In addition to the points listed above (all of which could be regarded as rewards), departments enjoying improved status and performance are better placed to be awarded bonuses, improved budgets and equipment, better and more office space, and so on. They also provide more senior managers with a range of benefits which will ensure the department has their support and approval.

Conclusions

From this brief examination you can see that there are a number of things to consider when looking at your customers. What influences their actions and experiences as a customer, and the opportunities to control or influence them, are directly linked to this.

Psychology is what drives or motivates the customer. It helps to define what they may be looking for or how they want to be approached or treated and what they are seeking behind the product or service. What we do when developing our product's or service's image, packaging, advertising and branding, communications and type/level of service may influence this. So, as we explore the various ways in which we can describe and define customers, we can keep asking what role will psychology play with these types of customers and with our type of product or service. We will also develop approaches to our business and internal customers as part of this process.

UNDERSTANDING CONSUMER PURCHASING

Every consumer is influenced by factors which change and vary in importance throughout their lives. These are some of the more important factors to consider when you try to understand who your customers are and what their buying motives might be:

- Gender
- Age
- Marital status
- Children in household
- Income
- Socio-economic groups
- Occupation
- Personal financial management

- Home ownership
- Location
- Life cycle/sagacity
- Geodemographic systems

Gender

Certain consumer products and services appear to be aimed at a specific sex, for example clothes or specialist health-care products. However, in reality, there are very few products or services which are not bought by both sexes.

Age

A consumer's age may provide some clues to their lifestyle and their interests. Products may be specifically targeted at an age group, for example retirement homes, Club 18–30 holidays, or the Puffin Book Club for children. Age groups are often grouped in decades starting at 15: 15–18, 18–20, 21–25, 25–34, 35–44, 45–54, 55–64, 65+.

Marital status

Marital status is a significant factor when it is combined with other factors such as children and income. Certain products or services may be aimed at people of a specific marital status, for example food and household products aimed at married couples, or small cars aimed at prosperous young single people. The categories are: single, married, divorced/separated, widowed.

Children in household

The presence of children in a household can have a significant effect on the disposable income of the household, its lifestyle, attitudes and consumption patterns. There is a vast difference in disposable income between single-income families with children and two-income families without children. The ages of the children also affects disposable income.

Income

Income is described in two ways – net or gross. Net income is after tax and any other basic living-costs have been deducted, whereas gross income is total income before tax and deductions. Not everyone is prepared to provide truthful answers about their income, so income is normally stated in £5000 or £10 000 bands. Lower income bands are often broken into smaller amounts to reflect the greater importance of an increase. The bands are: up to £5000, £5000–7500, £7500–10 000, £10 000–12 500, £12 500–15 000, £15 000–25 000, £25 000–35 000, £35 000–45 000, £45 000–55 000, £55 000–65 000, over £65 000.

Socio-economic groups

The socio-economic groups most commonly used in the UK were developed as a rationalization of social class in the 1950s. However, they are severely flawed both in their structure and in their value as a model of today's society. In 1981, the Market Research Society published an evaluation of social grades covering five socio-economic or social class groupings: A, B, C1, C2, D and E.

A   Higher managerial, administrative or professional.
B   Intermediate managerial, administrative or professional.
C1 Supervisory, clerical, junior administrative or professional.
C2 Skilled manual workers.
D   Semi-skilled and unskilled manual workers.
E   State pensioners, widows, casual and lowest-grade earners.

Occupation

Occupation is often too complex to help us discern its value as a factor in buying-behaviour. In fact, there are few pieces of research where the actual occupation is recorded, apart from the National Readership Survey. Most occupation research tends to use the same categories as socio-economic groupings. However, the research may also include information on the sector in which the respondent is employed, for example teaching, civil service, engineering or the professions.

Personal financial management

A consumer's use of credit and their approach to money can be useful factors in evaluating buying behaviour. Ownership of credit cards, and the number and type of bank and building society accounts are not just indicators of financial well-being, they may also have a bearing on the willingness or the ability of the consumer to purchase certain types of product or service.

Home ownership

Home ownership results in certain needs and responsibilities which correlate directly with purchasing patterns. Type of property owned, how long lived there and whether owned outright, or mortgaged and the size of mortgage all have a bearing on disposable income, aspirations, interests and other factors relating to buying behaviour.

Location

Where a consumer lives may have an important bearing on buying behaviour. Certain products or services may be limited to specific locations, and different cultural and economic factors may change from region to region. Rural and urban consumers differ, and there are also significant differences between city centre, council estate and suburban consumers.

MEDIA CONSUMPTION

The media we consume has long been a means of describing the sorts of people we are. Our images of what we are can be based more on assumption and myth than on fact. The specialists in this area (media researchers) tend to know a lot more about the people who are committed to specific media than the people who write or perform in them. The typical *Guardian* or *Telegraph* readers, for example, are likely to be substantially different to the people conjured up by the titles. *Guardian* readers will be more prosperous, more conventional and less liberal than expected and *Telegraph* readers more enlightened and younger.

Media researchers know all this because there is a considerable body of research into who consumes what media, when, how, why and how often. The basic findings are available in a number of libraries and can be easily found and studied so that you may have a better understanding of just exactly who is likely to read the *Sun* every day.

In addition to the general media we have an enormous wealth of other specialist media. Magazines and newspapers are supplemented by radio and TV programmes and stations, and by a plethora of web sites specializing in narrow and well-defined subjects. These provide clear access to people who, apart from any other characteristics they enjoy, can be classified according to their particular interests.

Very few people, for example, are likely to buy a helicopter pilot's magazine unless they have a deep interest in the subject. This is amplified greatly if the person actually subscribes to the publication.

While some of these media are based on self selection (not all helicopter pilots buy the magazine but all buyers of the magazine are, or are interested in becoming, helicopter pilots), others are based on membership. So all members of a professional body will receive the body's monthly journal but not all those interested in the profession will be qualified to receive a copy.

RELIGIOUS BELIEFS

Stereotyping and suffering from misleading myth and assumption have often been the lot suffered by those with religious beliefs and a commitment to a religion. Even when data about this has been asked, people have often been uncertain what to do with it. Recently (to coincide with the 2001 census) a major survey was carried out on the church-going population in England. With over 100 000 people surveyed, it is one of the largest privately commissioned market research surveys ever to take place within the UK.

The commercial report based on the survey 'Christian Citizens and Consumers' paints a picture which both redefines Christians as a market sector and indicates how those committed to a religion may differ from their secular counterparts in the population.

Two of the many defining and enlightening facts to emerge are that Christians are much more likely to donate to charities than the average person, and are committed volunteers active in their community. They are also heavy readers of quality daily and Sunday newspapers while being light TV viewers.

With active Christians accounting for over a quarter of the population, one can begin to consider just how important this group might

ACTION BOX 2.3

Using the same headings as in Action Box 2.2, try to list the key individual characteristics that best describe your customers or customer groups. Highlight what you believe to be the most significant characteristics and compare these with the motivations in the previous exercise. What does this tell you and can you now add or change any of the things listed either here or earlier?

be to different organizations. While they may actually be a major segment of some organization's markets, even if they are no more representative than they are in the population as a whole they may still constitute about 25% of your customers!

COMBINATIONS OF FACTORS

Our understanding of customers, their circumstances, their attitudes and behaviour comes from looking at more than one aspect of who they are. So, it is not enough to know that they are young, you need to know that the majority are also male; it's not enough to know that they are young men, you need to know that they have a lot of money to spend, and so on.

For many years the only way to combine factors was to have a large enough survey (both in numbers of respondents and in numbers of questions) to provide you with the ability to look at smaller groups in more detail and combine lots of different factors. This invariably meant that a group of similar organizations needed to get together and share data. Hence the large readership and other media surveys and data sources such as TGI (Target Group Index), which looks at how and what people buy.

With the development of geodemographic systems (see below) and the greater power of computers it is now possible to combine factors from a variety of sources reliably and effectively.

Combinations from single sources

Each of the different types of sources tells us something about the sorts of data that have become important to businesses and how businesses have seen or developed images of customers over the years.

From surveys

Basic combinations attempting to bring key information together to make a clear and informative picture of customers has led to a variety of descriptive models of society. Traditional ones such as 'Sagacity' (developed by the research company RSL Ltd) attempted to describe consumers according to the stage of their life (single young people, newly married, married with children, etc.). Although helpful in some marketing situations, criticisms of this approach include their highly traditional view or biased assumptions about society (ignoring gay couples, single parents, and so on) based on the sorts of markets the designers seemed to be most interested in.

Newer developments added more colour to the combinations and used a less proscriptive approach. In this case the researchers used statistical techniques in order to group similar people together across a wide range of factors, and then interpreted the results rather than having a predetermined model of society and trying to fit as many people into it as possible. The results of such an approach have proven very useful. Through the use of mainly demographic data the famous 'yuppies' (young, upwardly mobile people) were born and a whole set of new approaches to marketing were heralded.

Using large psychologically based surveys, the same sort of approach was used to develop groups of people with different approaches to the world around them. Lifestyle and psychographic classifications of people resulted from this (see section earlier on this). The importance of some of these was the way in which researchers have applied them. The research defining the different groups uses a very large bank of questions but once the groups have been identified the researchers can select a much smaller number of key questions that will help them identify people in each of the different groups quite accurately. So, instead of having to add tens if not hundreds of questions to a given questionnaire in order to combine the classification with the marketing research, they only needed to add ten or twenty key questions. Marketers could then examine how people classed as early adopters of new technology were likely to react to their new product or track how different groups bought over a period of time.

However, it still did not allow researchers to combine the results of different surveys together reliably.

From the census

Census data has been in use since the end of the 1970s to group together places where similar types of people live. By the early 1980s this was being done using census data at enumeration district (ED) level (the area covered by a census enumerator – approximately 150 households) and these EDs were being used to assign characteristics to postal codes. So, in very simple terms, all the postal codes located within a very posh ED were assumed to be postcodes where posh people lived.

This meant that the publicly available electoral roll could be used as a mailing list where all the people with particular postcodes could be targeted for direct mail, leafleting or sales purposes. And, because there were surveys being carried out where all of the respondents could be coded up in the same way, marketers could measure the likelihood of each group to buy a given product or service. Groups with the highest propensity to buy were then targeted.

The first and arguably the best known system of this sort is ACORN (A Classification of Residential Neighbourhoods). Systems of this sort are called geodemographic classification systems. 'Geo' because they are to do with places, 'demographic' because they use demographic data such as age, gender, income, and so on, from the census and they classify areas systematically according to how similar they are to each other across a wide range of different factors.

These systems were welcomed as more reliable partly because the similarities between people in different areas can be measured, and so can their differences; their behaviour is also measurably different. Also attractive was the fact that the systems can be used to analyse databases containing postcodes but with no usable or comparable data about the people on the database, and they can be used to select respondents for well-balanced representative samples. In the past, research agencies used social class as a major element in the sample but respondents were selected by, and their classification based on, the judgement of the interviewer along with some very basic filter questions. ACORN and its sister systems meant that you could remove a lot of bias by selecting sample points within selected and classified areas.

Today, as links with postcodes have improved and as techniques get better, more and more variations of these systems have been developed – some specializing in serving the financial industry, others for particular large companies, and so on.

Lifestyle data sources

The last 20 years have seen the development and growth of a number of database marketing companies who specialize in amassing and manipulating very large datasets of consumers. They are not in the business of compiling census data but, rather, as large and as up-to-date a bank of information on consumers as possible. They gather data through guarantee cards, shopper surveys and a number of other techniques, and they combine basic demographic data with shopping preferences and actual purchase data, and with data on what respondents like to do and are interested in. The last type of information is described as lifestyle data and these databases are generally known as lifestyle databases.

With more up-to-date and more market-oriented information than the census, and with more reliable names and addresses than expected from most electoral rolls, these data sources have been able to provide a wide range of marketing services.

Other data sources

Other large data sources include data on households and individuals which would never have been used or been available in the past. The range is vast, from who has County court judgments against them, to the value, type and size of your house, but most are of more value when combined with other data than used on their own.

Mega combinations

Not surprisingly, geodemographic classification systems and lifestyle databases are being used more in unison with each other than as competing systems. They enhance each other and allow marketers the ability to analyse, segment and target more effectively. They are also used within the context of surveys, to analyse sets of customer or respondent names and addresses, to plan and target advertising and retail distribution, and a myriad other uses. They are also used by

---

ACTION BOX 2.4

Using what information you have access to about external customers, experiment to see how you might put together combinations to best describe your key customer groups. What might the combinations tell you that individual characteristics miss and how does it help to define a bigger group of important customers? Or do your combinations end up as ever-decreasing groups of customers? What does this tell you?

Now look at how your organization currently approaches the issue of combining customer characteristics. Do you have access to sophisticated or well-tested information in this area or has it not been a priority or significant part of your organization's approach? If you do have access to this sort of information, spend some time getting to grips with both what it tells you and how it was put together. If no information exists, what does this tell you and how should you respond to this?

large organizations to classify the population into groups more relevant to their sector than the generic classifications could ever be.

CUSTOMERS IN YOUR ORGANIZATION

In order to see internal markets and customers in a useful way we need to understand our situation better. We need to identify what we can influence, what changes we can make, and then work out what effect these might have on our customers and ourselves.

Understanding your internal markets

First, internal markets usually do not operate in the same way as external ones. The exchanges within the external market may not be determined by cost in the same way, and the amount of demand or usage may be determined by a different concept of need. Your internal customers may not be able to choose anyone other than you for the given product or service you provide. Financial costs and the level and types of usage made of your products or services will be determined by the organization and its priorities rather than by the individuals involved.

Second, those elements will usually determine who your customers are and may even cause you and your department to be seen in a particular way.

Third, what you provide will be a key element in the way in which the relationship works.

Finally, your role and position within the organization, and your position relative to your customers, may also affect both their attitude and use of your products and services and the way in which you and your staff operate.

ACTION BOX 2.5

The following section can be used either as a guide to how to think of your internal customers or as part of your Action Box activities. The information you gather in this section will become a database of information on your internal customers, so keep a separate sheet or file for each customer you analyse. To compile the database for your workbook, follow the instructions below.

Building a better understanding of your customers

First, decide who your internal customers are. Writing a list of your internal customers may open your eyes to exactly what you are doing as well as who you are doing things for within your organization. Try to list every person and department you provide services, information, goods, materials, equipment, advice and support to. It does not matter how long the list is; it needs to be comprehensive. Keep this as a master list as you will want to add people and departments to it as you continue to consider this while reading this book, and you may have to change the list as time goes on and your organization or role changes.

Using your list as a starting point, consider the following for each individual or departmental customer:

What are you expected to provide and what do they get? This is where you can consider what you and your department are expected to provide. As you examine this you may find that circumstances, history or some other reason has caused you and your department to provide more (or less) than is actually specified. For example, you may be required to provide the customer with a basic set of information, but with improvements in your own practices or in technology it is now possible to provide a lot more information, and so that is what you do. In other circumstances it may be the case that it was never practical to provide everything specified and so neither party expects more. Perhaps you or your department have decided, at some stage, to exceed your customer's expectations or the expectations are impossible given your current resources.

Whatever the details are, write down a brief note of what you are expected to provide, what you actually provide and a summary of why.

Is there an alternative source? It may be the case that you provide all of the stationery or computers to the organization but that it is possible for individual departments to source their own; or you may be the only source with what they want.

How does this contribute to the organization? Consider how serving this customer helps to advance the aims of the organization as a whole. It may be a small thing, but it may be important, or it may simply contribute in a more general way to the organization's success.

How often do you serve this customer? In addition to considering the frequency of this you should also look at *how much* time and effort you spend on this.

What do you/your department get in return and from whom? It may be that there is no obvious and direct benefit coming from the customer to you in return for your service. Indirectly, you may be able to say that part of your department's budget has been paid in exchange for this and you may also be able to take into account goodwill not only from the customers you serve but also from various managers and other departments.

What sort of relationship is there here? Do you or your staff enjoy the relationship you have with this customer and how does it affect the rest of the work you or they do? Does your customer enjoy the relationship and can you describe the feelings/attitudes experienced by both parties here?

Pulled out any stops lately? Have you done anything exceptional or helped out that customer recently? What was it and why did it happen? Was it to help them or retrieve yourself or department from a difficult situation? What was the outcome, has it changed your customer's perception or attitude towards you?

How important to you is this? Can you rank your customer in relation to all of your other internal customers? You may want to look at all of them in some detail before you decide this.

What is your customer's position within the organization/department? and

What is your customer's position relative to your or your department's position? You will need to consider these together as it will help you decide how the relative positions affect the way in which you regard your customers and they regard you and/or your department. It will also help you place them in the context of your other customers.

If you work your way through all of these questions for each of your internal customers, you will be able to identify who your most important customers are and why, but you will also be able to see just how much time and effort is spent on each customer. It will become clear that even smaller, apparently less important customers can have a major impact on what you do. It will also be clear that the links between morale and customer relationships are very strong. From this work you will be able to identify three customers you could serve better with measurable improvements in yourself and your department's position and productivity.

CUSTOMERS IN THE BUYER COMPANY

Figure 1.9 in Chapter 1 identifies six different types of potential customer within a client organization. This was to help you see how the path to customers could also be mirrored by the buyer's path within the customer or client organization. Expanding each of these categories within the company's buying process, you can begin to see how understanding the process of serving internal customers might help you improve your response to the needs of business customers.

ACTION BOX 2.6

Identify the best and the worst supplier your organization currently uses (as judged by those who are in the best position to know). Compare how your organization interacts with these companies. Try to identify those people in your company who best fit the categories set out above (users, deciders, gatekeepers, etc.) and find out how they react to and interact with the two suppliers. Is there a difference in both the number of categories involved in dealing with each supplier and how well the system works for the parties involved? How can you apply what you have learned to the way in which you and your department operate as suppliers?

CUSTOMERS DEFINED BY THE RELATIONSHIP

There are a number of ways in which you can classify your customers based on different aspects of their relationship to you. We have already explored how the positions and roles of your internal customers affect your relationships with them and seen how patterns of behaviour can affect relationships with external customers. It is now time to explore this further.

Aspects of the relationship

The way in which you and your organization work and interact with customers is important. We have looked at some of this already, and here you should consider the idea explored in Chapter 1 where you looked at how many opportunities your customers have to be in con-

Users	These people initiate purchase, buy it and use it. You may have most initial direct contact with this group but they may not be the ones who have the final say or the money to buy. They need good information and lots of support to help them sell your products or services to the people inside their organization. Customer service and after-sales support may be seen as a personal benefit to them while it may be a financial and efficiency-related issue to others.
Influencers	As the name suggests, these people influence, provide information, evaluate alternatives and may be technical or similar staff. These may be the people who need to visit your HQ, manufacturing plant, support unit or whatever. Along with more detailed technical and other specifications, this group needs to be shown demonstrably high levels of skill and knowledge. They like people who are like themselves. They need support to help them write favourable reports.
Deciders	They are the ones who have the power to make the buying decision. They may be less technically knowledgeable although you cannot assume this to be the case. They are less interested in detail but want proper reassurance. Your organization's credibility, reliability, sound financial footings, and their access to easily accessible information to help them always appear knowledgeable are all important to them.
Approvers	This group authorizes the proposed decisions. Similar in many ways to Deciders but may have little or nothing to do with the product or service itself. They might be financial managers or senior managers with little time for details and a need to see the strategic context and the top-line results. Your help with the other groups and the supporting information should include the most useful information for this group as well. It may be the case that one of this group will be interested in developing a relationship with their equivalent in your organization or it may be useful to provide details so that a senior manager in the client company will have the opportunity to discover that someone they know is a senior manager in your organization.
Buyers	Buyers have the formal authority to select vendors, be involved in negotiations and buy. If your client company has someone whose sole purpose is to do specialist buying for their organization, you will find that they are extremely knowledgeable both about what they are buying and who they can buy from. As well as being important customers requiring good information and support, good relationships with them may provide useful competitor information.
Gatekeepers	People between sellers and the buying and other related departments. They may be receptionists, secretaries, etc. Important people to have a good relationship with and, in certain cases, your support may help them move on to other positions where they could influence buying decisions even more. Selling may be impossible if they act as a barrier.

Figure 2.2
Type of customer within a client organization.

tact with you. There is a great difference between customers who only interface with the organization when there is a problem and those who are presented with a variety of opportunities to be in contact.

The number of different points of contact are as important as the types of contact, but the relationship is also defined by the number of customers you might have. A multinational bank with a local branch may have its image affected by the experience of customers regularly using the branch and having mundane interactions with familiar local staff. In contrast, a smaller internet and telephone-based bank may be more convenient but have a different image because of the less frequent personal contact and the lack of human, face-to-face inter-actions experienced by its customers. Both will meet personal needs and tastes while presenting images to their customers that may be very different from their actual core business.

A more obvious difference in customer experience might be a business and a personal banking customer. The same bank may have an individual dealing personally with the business account, while serving the personal account holder through a call centre.

The smaller the number of customers an organization deals with, the more detailed and intimate the relationship can be. This makes it possible to develop stronger and more complex relationships but it also provides different risks, too. A relationship that is more impor-tant to both parties can be heavily dependent on particular indivi-duals. The loss of one such individual from an organization can be expensive and painful. Furthermore, the more significant the relation-ship, the greater the damage caused by even relatively small failures experienced in it.

The choices customers have

Although it may appear simple, choice does affect how your cus-tomers approach your products and services.

The most obvious choice issue is availability. If competing products are in the market place but the customers of your products do not have access to these, a feeling of resentment may affect the relation-ship. A common example of this is the local shop where only those who are mobile or have the time to use public transport or who can afford it will have access to alternatives. Those without choice will often feel that they are being taken advantage of even when this is not the case.

Similar outcomes may result from geographic limits to distribution or where only those with access to the Internet or who have credit cards can take advantage of the alternatives on offer.

Of course, choice may not simply be about access and availability. If people can only afford the cheapest they may feel that real choice has been denied them.

There are a number of other ways restrictions in choice can be experienced by customers. With many of them comes a sense of being denied the alternative, and a feeling that this has led them to be short-changed or missing something better.

Interestingly, if we look to the very exclusive and expensive end of the market we will invariably find that limited choice and high prices mark out the quality and exclusivity of the product or service to the customer. It can often be useful to look closely at that extreme in your own market-place (if it exists) and ask yourself how you could incorporate aspects of what you find there into your own activities.

Frequency of buying/using

Customers can be classified by how often they buy or use products or services. For example, media owners define audiences by this aspect of their behaviour. People who watch a large amount of TV every day are different from those who seldom watch. Their lifestyles, age, income and education can all be reflected in their behaviour and as each group is attractive to different advertisers, how you use the media to reach them is defined by how they consume the media.

Frequency of usage patterns can help you to understand different groups better. For example, the level of purchase of washing powder will reflect the size and type of household, and changes in household patterns will cause manufacturers to rethink products.

Frequency of purchase can also help marketers to classify different types of potential customer. So, direct marketers value a list of people who are 'known responders' over most other types of list because the people on the list have a record of regularly or often buying in a particular way. Their past behaviour defines their potential for the future.

Frequency also helps to define people as customers. If a person buys once you will try to encourage them to buy again. If they are buying regularly from you, the next step is to try to define how much of their needs are being met by your organization in comparison with other organizations. Your objective will be to increase their purchase to the point where you are the exclusive supplier, and so on.

So, frequency defines them as a customer, and customers with purchases declining in frequency are ones that need to be investigated, nurtured and reintroduced to what your organization can provide.

The issues surrounding loyalty do relate to frequency, value, etc., but we will treat this as a full subject and explore it in a later chapter (see Chapter 9).

Value

Often linked with frequency is the value of purchases made by a customer. It is important to be able to identify people who can and do spend at different levels of value as well as by the frequency of purchases. Obviously, your product or service might have a direct influence on how patterns are made and interpreted, but value is usually of great importance when looking at how to segment customers.

In many markets you will find that a large proportion of the value of your sales will be accounted for by a relatively small proportion of your customers. A number of marketers have argued that you should concentrate most of your effort on the group of customers representing the greatest value to you. Reward schemes based on frequent air travel are based on this approach. In contrast, reward schemes with major retail groups tend to reward all who shop with the group and provide greater benefits as purchasing levels increase. Each may be appropriate to their markets and appear to be designed to win and develop business with specific customers at the expense of competitors.

Age of relationship

The age of the relationship with your customer is also linked to value and frequency. Until recently, only specific types of businesses could track and record customers and thereby identify long term versus short term ones. Indeed, some companies failed to see the relevance of this. However, it is extremely important and many businesses develop strategies and plans based around reducing what is called the 'attrition rate' which is the rate at which you lose and have to replace customers. The fewer customers lost, and the longer someone stays your customer, the healthier your prospects. So, being able to classify customers according to the age of their relationship with you is important as it will tell you a lot about the health of your business as well as about your customers.

Competition

We looked briefly at competition in Chapter 1. How your customers compare with your competitors' customers and how much of your customer base is shared with your competitors helps to put a lot of your analysis in perspective. If you share the same target markets as your competitors you will need to understand how well you are doing against various aspects of market share (numbers, volume, value, etc.). How you fit within the general market-place and where your organization intends to be in a few years' time will also be important. How the market place views you and your competitors will help you make some of the decisions you will need to take in order to reach your objectives, and monitoring comparative positions will help you know if you are on track and how well you are really doing.

Understanding the links between different products and services within the market place will also be helpful. It may be that some of your competitors' products or services are actually complementary with yours. Some manufacturers, for example, regard purchase of competitors' products a necessary precursor to purchase of their own. Some car manufacturers and many camera and audio equipment manufacturers frequently see new customers coming from the ranks of those who buy cheaper versions of their own products. Such purchasers are aspiring customers who build knowledge and develop the preferences and desires necessary to prepare them for the higher end of the market.

Satisfaction and loyalty, as indicated above, will be looked at in detail in Chapter 8 & 9.

Where do you find your customers?

Where your customers find out about your organization and decide to become customers can be very useful. It will add to your knowledge of what they do, which media they use and may even give you insights into their buying behaviour. It will also help you find other similar customers.

This is why every properly designed direct-response advertisement provides the advertiser with information on where and when the person responding saw the advertisement. In published media there is usually a code of some sort, all scripts for telephone response handlers should ask the questions, and on-line response forms should also ask where and when.

ACTION BOX 2.7

Divide your page into two columns with the headings 'Customers' and 'Choices' and then, starting with your domestic customers (followed by business and then internal customers) write down the sort of choices available to each of your customers or customer groupings. Which customers in each category share the same types of choices and how else are they similar? Conversely, how can you differentiate between them based on their choices and what does that tell you about your customers? Use all of the choice categories above and explore other choices not mentioned here.

Conclusions – balancing interests internally and externally

This chapter is just scratching the surface to show you what you can and will find out about your customers. Once you begin looking you will find more and more that needs to be understood. However, one of the key skills of a good manager is being able to successfully balance a wide range of interests and this is what we will be exploring next.

With so much to understand and make use of it should always be possible to find complementary ways of meeting your different customer needs. By improving internal communications you will help ensure better service to customers, and by improving your understanding of customer needs you will have more effective advertising which will boost sales, and so on. However, without a good knowledge and understanding of our customers we will find it hard to know what to improve and develop so that we can reach our goals effectively.

Competence self-assessment

1 For each level of Maslow's hierarchy of needs, name a well-known product or service that fits the need or uses that level to promote or accentuate the product/service's values.
2 Identify three major differences in the decision-making process leading to the purchase of a holiday or a car by a family, a couple and a single person. How do the motivations as well as the processes differ between each type of purchasing category?

3 List four important changes that have taken place since the 1970s that have changed the population and their circumstances. How have these changes affected both the way that customers act and what they buy?

4 Select a department in your organization that you feel is as good as or better than your own and identify the key aspects that single it out as a very good department. How many of these aspects should be adopted by all departments and how might that affect the organization as a whole?

5 Choose a well-known brand or product/service in each of the following categories (cars, holidays, cleaning products, breakfast cereals) and list the characteristics of their customers. How does each company express the characteristics you choose in their advertising?

6 Prepare a profile of the head of the department that you have identified as your most important internal customer.

7 Identify circumstances when you might act as a User, Influencer, Decider, Approver, Buyer and Gamekeeper. Name one thing that would positively influence you while you are in each role.

8 Select the retailer you do most of your weekly shopping with or are most familiar with. Consider the choices you have as their customer and identify what the most important ones are to you. When did you last consider where to concentrate most of your shopping and has your view of the store now changed? What will they have to do to keep your custom?

9 What proportion of your department's efforts is devoted to serving your external customers directly versus indirectly? Name the one change that would most positively affect the customer's experience of your organization.

REFERENCES

Kotler, P. (1988) *The Principles of Marketing, Analysis, Planning, Implementation and Control* (6th edn). New Jersey: Prentice Hall.

Maslow, A. H. (1954) *Motivation and Personality*. New York: Harper & Row.

Mitchell, A. (1983) *The Nine American Lifestyles*. New York: Macmillan.

CHAPTER 3

The route to your customers

The route is a physical and a mental journey. The impact of attitudes and priorities along the path can affect how products and services are experienced at point of delivery. Distance from origin to delivery is also important and relates to cost and control as well as access to key information. How can the route and the other elements be combined to make sense of the whole process? How can individuals and departments affect this and plan to play their parts in improved success?

We had an opportunity in Chapter 1 to look at how the route to customers affects the whole process of meeting customer needs. We have also had the chance to look at our customers in more detail and now have a number of different ways of recognizing them and understanding how they might act in relation to our products or services. In this chapter we will take the time to take a closer look at the route, how it operates and what sort of influences we can exert along the way.

REVIEWING THE ROUTE SO FAR

So far we have recognized that there are barriers between our customers and ourselves. We have seen that distance is important, as are the degrees and types of contact and the involvement of and types of relationship between the customer and organization.

In this chapter we will extend these ideas by exploring their emotional, physical, indirect and incomplete aspects. You will soon be addressing planning and strategic issues relating to meeting customer needs and here is where you will start to look at how the priorities relate to each other and how you can make sense of apparent conflicts while balancing the different demands made on you and your department.

ACTION BOX 3.1

Using your current knowledge and by simply asking other departments, score each department in your organization according to the proportion of its time and effort spent working with or for the organization's external customers, and time/effort spent working with or for your department. If you use a 5-point scale, 1 could represent virtually no time or effort spent and 5 would be virtually all of their time and effort spent.

Assign each department a letter and create a matrix with the vertical side titled 'Involvement with customers' and the horizontal side 'Involvement with my department'. You can now map out the departments in your organization by their involvement with you and the customers. What does this tell you about your own department and the departments in your organization?

Physical routes in more detail

How close are you to your organization's customers? Do you deal with them directly or do you serve/support those who do? Do you manage systems or processes that have no discernible links with external customers? Does your organization only serve other organizations, who in their turn have connections with end-users that you might describe as external customers? With each question comes a set of possible images of what your organization is like and where you fit into it.

Revisiting the map

Let us start by confirming who your organization's customers actually are and what your customers get.

This may seem relatively simple if you work for a manufacturer of consumer goods or for a retailer or a financial services company, etc.

If you work for the police or the Civil Service you will have discovered by now that you have customers who might be the general public or some subset of them. You may also have the Government or the judiciary as another customer and perhaps a minister or minister's department, or other bodies (a hospital might have the health authority, GPs, other medical professionals and the Department of Health as customers while teachers might have the Department for Education, Local Authorities, and so on).

The point is that you should be considering who your customers are, what they get from you and the route that it takes from its originating point(s) to the customer. If that means you have to acknowledge that the service is a combined effort from the organization as a whole that is fine; if you see the end-customer as being the general public but your organization serves them through your work for a government minister, so be it; if you are a prison warden and you serve the public through delivering secure accommodation and training to convicted criminals, that is a good start.

Using the explorations we have already made we can put together a simple table with the following headings: Source(s), Points passed, Direct customer contacts and Customers (see Figure 3.1). When filling in such a table it is often easier to start with the customers and work your way back, then after filling it out for all of your different customer groups you can test the route by going from source to customer. Each column needs some thought:

Figure 3.1
Elements of the
route to
customers.

Source(s)	Points passed	Direct customer contacts	Customers

Customers

How do you wish to define your organization's customers? If you run the book-keeping for a large restaurant, your company's most obvious customers will be the diners in the restaurant; but you may also provide contract catering services for various types of functions outside the restaurant, for private parties in restaurants and in people's homes, etc. The contractor in some cases will be the customer but your success will be judged on how well you serve the contractor's customers.

Direct customer contacts

Once we begin to look at the different types of customers we often begin to see that there is more than one flow or route through the system. So, direct contact with diners in the restaurant will be with the staff serving in the restaurant, from initial booking through to receiving payment and thanking the customers for their custom. Customers in the contract catering activity may be the sales people from the restaurant, the chef and other management staff and the finance and administrative departments. The end-customers (i.e. the diners at the conference dinner) may be served by temporary or casual waiters who are, in turn, managed by one person or a small team from the restaurant. The supervising waiting staff and the chef's team might never be seen or known by the diners.

Points passed

This is all of the parts of the organization not directly interfacing with the customers. You can, as we have done, subdivide this into two columns to denote the ones closest to and those most remote from direct contact with the customers. So, those involved in preparing the different aspects of the service provided at the restaurant will be in the section closest to the 'Direct customer contact' column (for example, various cooking staff, those in charge of specialist food/drink-related functions, etc.) while staff supporting this group and other administrative roles (e.g. accounts/book-keeping, marketing, cleaning, buying, maintenance, etc.) may be placed in the other column.

Source(s)

There may be a number of different organizations where it might be difficult to clearly identify the final source of a product or service, and that is quite alright. Sometimes there will be several main contributors or contributing sources, but in our example the strongest candidates are the chef and the proprietor although other people may be eligible as additional sources (one or more senior directors, the Maitre d', and so on).

Converting this into route maps is simplified if we only take one product or service at a time. Figure 3.2 is an example of how the restaurant takes the original meals and special ambience of the restaurant from the source (its chef and proprietor) to the customers (restaurant diners) and shows where the manager of the book-keeping

Figure 3.2
Example of the restaurant – elements of their route to customers.

Source(s)	Points passed		Direct customer contacts	Customers
Chef	HR support	Cooking staff	Maitre d'	Diners
Proprietor	Buying	Under chefs, etc.	Waiting staff	
Other senior management	Maintenance	Cellar staff	Wine and other staff	Contractors
	Marketing			Events and other companies, etc.
	Cleaners		Booking dept.	
	Accounts		Till staff	
	Decorators			

department fits into the whole process. Note how the direct customers of the book-keeping department are all directly linked, but some flow on towards the external customer and others flow back before they flow outwards again.

ACTION BOX 3.2

Using the notes above put together your own version of Figure 3.1 for your organization and use Figure 1.6 to help you construct a new customer route map. If this is not possible, or you wish to practice, use the information in Figure 3.2 to construct a map for the restaurant business.

Inputs and outputs

With these tables and maps in front of us, showing us how the players are placed within the process it is possible for us to begin to identify what is flowing between each of the parts in the diagram. What are the department's inputs (what it receives from other departments) and what are its outputs (what it produces and provides to other departments)?

A by-product of compiling this list will be to check that nothing has been missed in the diagram. However, the most important outcome will be a clearer idea of what you actually produce, who it is for and what is done with it. From the list you should be able to see how your department's activities contribute to the process of meeting customer needs.

Figure 3.3 takes our example of the book-keeping department in the restaurant and explores how the inputs and outputs might work.

Although the book-keeping department seldom sees a customer and feels quite separate from the delivery of services, the list soon

Inputs: *from*	Outputs: *to*

Transactions: Chefs
  : Cellar master
  : Maitre d'
  : Proprietor
  : Maintenance
  : Human resources
  : Marketing
  : Contract sales staff, etc.
Information: All departments
  : Accounts dept
  : Human resources
  : Contract sales
  : Events organizers
	Payments: External suppliers
	  : Staff
	  : Contractors
	  : Inland Revenue, etc.
	  : Landlord
	  : Local Authority
	  : Professional bodies
	  : Media owners/ad agencies
	  : Service/utility suppliers, etc.
	
	Confirm payment: All depts
	
	Accounts: Accounts dept
	  : Senior management
	Refunds: Customers

Figure 3.3
Extract from the book-keeper's input/output table.

begins to show how much of a hub it is for certain types of activity. Although the inputs and outputs appear repetitive they each have their own defined characteristics and each is essential to the smooth running of the restaurant. Without prompt and proper payment of bills the restaurant will not be able to guarantee its supply of vital produce, it will not be able to price and plan menus without clear and accurate details of costs, and so on. The quality of the food and the commitment of staff and suppliers can be traced partly to the good work of the book-keeping department. In a small restaurant these tasks may have been carried out by the chef and proprietor but the complexity and volume of book-keeping for a large restaurant means that it should be left to specialists.

The list also helps us in our expanding information about internal customers setting them in the context of the organization as a whole and showing how the internal market is more a process of exchange rather than one-way flows. We often need inputs from those internal customers before we can provide them with the necessary outputs.

ACTION BOX 3.3

Compile your own input/output table trying to be as exhaustive as possible. Familiarity can cause you to devalue the worth or importance of regular activities. Are there any inputs you could really do without and, of the outputs least important to you and your department, which are also not important to the departments that receive them?

EMOTIONAL ROUTES

We examined some aspects of the emotional routes when we were looking at the 'buyer behaviour' of our customers in Chapter 2. The emotional route is one taken by our customers to us but the route is our responsibility – we should be maintaining this route but few of us even consider it.

The route starts with *customer motivation* (their need or desire for the product or service, driving them to seek it), the *image* of the product or service (what we present to them), their *expectations and experience* (how we promise and deliver), their *comparisons* (our products or services compared with our competitors) and their *attitudes* (their resultant feelings towards us and our products or services).

Figure 3.4 presents this route and shows how you and your competitors exert influence along it.

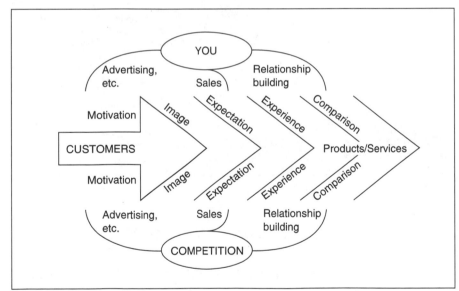

Figure 3.4
The emotional
route map.

WHERE DOES MOTIVATION LIE?

We already know something about our customers – who they are, what they are like, etc. What we also have to think about is what they are seeking from us. We have our view of what we are providing but do they share this view? We need to look at this idea of a product or service in more detail to understand what our customers might be thinking.

Figure 3.5 suggests that products or services are three things. They are made up of a *Core*, a *Tangible* and an *Augmented* product or service.

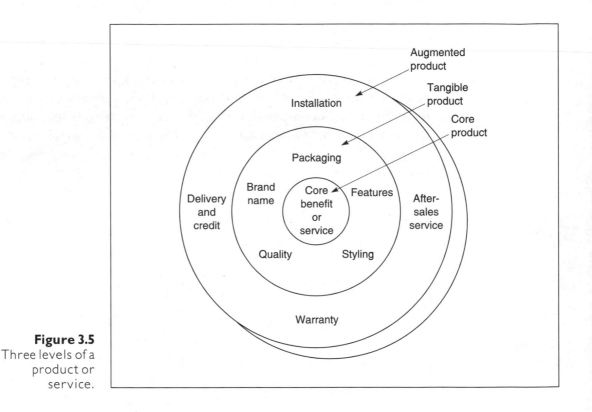

Figure 3.5
Three levels of a product or service.

The Core product or service

The core product of the Royal Mail is not stamps or courier services or even the postal system. It is the means of solving communications problems cheaply and effectively. Do toothpaste manufacturers only sell toothpaste? They sell protection from tooth decay and they 'sell' clean, fresh mouths. They identify the needs, fears and hopes of their customers and their products are designed to overcome their customers' concerns. Similarly, your internal customers may not view what you offer in the way you see it. Take time to think of what you, as an internal customer, think you are getting from your major suppliers. Now you can ask yourself what your department's and your organization's core products or services are.

The Tangible product or service

Tangible products are those things that satisfy your customer's needs or wants. So if you were manufacturing toothpaste you could list the following:

- The product's composition.
- Its design.
- The quality of its ingredients.
- Dispenser design.
- Packaging design.
- Research and development skills.
- General staff expertise.
- Staff attitude and commitment.
- Its brand name and reputation.
- The brand logo and identity.
- The instructions.
- The manufacturer's reputation.

You could also list specific details about your brand that would be linked with the Tangible product or service elements:

- Available in a variety of sizes.
- Sold in three different styles of dispenser.
- Available in three different flavours.
- Its ingredients are hypo-allergenic.
- Quality controls are better than any other manufacturer.
- The brand is available in all leading stores, supermarkets and chemists, as well as in the majority of minor retail outlets.
- The tubes and other dispensers are environmentally friendly.
- The product is not tested on animals.

The Augmented product or service

This is the part of the product or service which adds value to it – for example, a guarantee or a free advice service, an extended warranty or a discount on the next consultation. In the example of the toothpaste, the augmented product might include the following:

- The company has a dental help-line for all of its customers.
- It has a money-back guarantee system if the customer is not satisfied with the product.

- It works with individual dentists and dental organizations on dental care education.
- It has a set of school dental-education packs for different age groups.
- It carries out research on teeth, dental decay and techniques.
- It funds several scholarships and awards.

So the emotional route is one that starts with what the customer is seeking. Our understanding of this should help us guide customers towards us and provide them with what they are seeking.

If we can reach our potential customers by knowing who they are and where we might find them and if we know what they are looking for in terms that go beyond their mechanical descriptions we can put together a message that will present the *image* that fits what they are looking for. The closer you are to what they want, the greater your chance of winning them as customers.

ACTION BOX 3.4

Using the product or service you chose in Action Box 3.2, list all of its attributes for each of the levels above. Then compare these with what you know of your closest competitors' products/services. Which attributes set yours apart from the competition? Where do these important differences lie? Are they in the Core, Tangible or Augmented levels?

After considering the Core and the Tangible and the Augmented aspects of what you offer, you will be able to come to terms with what your customers are really looking for when they come to you and your organization. The customer view of this was once expressed in this way:

Do not offer me things.

Do not offer me clothes. Offer me attractive looks.

Do not offer me shoes. Offer me comfort for my feet and the pleasure of walking.

Do not offer me books. Offer me hours of pleasure and the benefit of knowledge.

Do not offer me records. Offer me leisure and the sound of music.

Do not offer me furniture. Offer me comfort and the quietness of a cosy place.

> Do not offer me things. Offer me ideas, emotions, feelings and benefits.
> Please do not offer me things.

So *image* and *need* are characteristics that help to develop the *attitudes* customers have towards potential suppliers. You will recognize this in shoppers who never buy in a particular store because they believe it to sell cheap or shoddy produce – even when they have never shopped there. Another example might be those who never consider buying a particular product because they believe it to be overpriced or out of their price range – and their belief stops them from even taking a look at the prices and products of that manufacturer. Often, the image presented by the company in question is a major source or strong reinforcer of the image in the customer's mind.

From our presentation of what we have to offer (such as our advertising and marketing efforts), potential customers develop *expectations*. Again, each customer will make decisions based on a wide range of needs and circumstances but what they expect from you and your organization will be directly linked to what you have told them to expect. The Moment Of Truth (MOT) occurs in the relationship when they *experience* what you have to offer. This is when you have to at least meet and hopefully exceed your customer's expectations. This is where you (or your organization) and your product or service meets face to face with the customer – the point where a potential customer becomes an actual customer.

You can expect the outcome of this MOT to define the rest of your relationship with your customer. If you revisit Chapter 1, Figure 1.3, you will recall how expectation and experience affect customers. The emotional route your customers might take if they are disappointed is away from you and once they turn away it is much harder to persuade them to turn back. Emotional memory is powerful. To prove this to yourself try to recall a time when you said to yourself, 'I'll never go back there again' after experiencing disappointing service or bad treatment. Have you ever returned, and why?

So the image builds attitudes and expectations while experience modifies them into a personal vision of what your organization and products/services mean to the customer.

The final aspect of the emotional route taken by customers is their compulsion to compare what they have with what was and is now on offer. This desire to compare is regularly seen when media owners conduct research on people's interest in and recall of advertising within their medium. The research reveals a strong link between high interest in advertising and recency of purchase. For example, many of those interested in car advertisements have recently bought a car, interest in washing machine ads is likely to denote recent purchase of one, and so on.

Further research reveals that these people are both checking out what they could have bought and some are reassuring themselves that they made a good decision. However, those who were unhappy about their experience are looking at what they should have bought and reinforcing their decision never to buy from the disappointing source company again.

ACTION BOX 3.5

Create a table with the five stages on the emotional route map as column headings. Now collect all the information you can about the product or service in previous Action Boxes. Which forms of communication/interaction with your customers will be most effective in influencing customers at each stage? What other actions might also be effective?

INDIRECT CONTACTS

There are a variety of indirect routes you might have to your customer. The sections covering your customer's route to you identified some of them and they also appear in your explorations of the physical routes to customers. However, they are significant enough to be worth looking at briefly here.

Indirect contacts are those routes or parts of the route that involve no direct interaction or interface between the organization and the customer.

The retail conundrum

For a number of organizations these are important when the customer sees the whole buying process up to transaction and on to after-sales care as being the sole remit of another organization such as the retailer. The wider the gap is between the customer and producer, the harder it is to establish a relationship.

Some companies try to overcome this by having a very strong relationship with their retailer partners. Some go further by incorporating their brand into the retailer's even when there is no basis for this in terms of ownership. And there are companies and whole sectors where retail outlets become the sole preserve of particular brands. This is typical in the car industry with its dealerships but it is also noticeable in public houses, etc. However, control of the emotional elements discussed earlier may still be out of the manufacturer's hands.

Marketing effort expended by companies who rely on retailers and have no direct selling capability of their own is often split between the promotion of their products/brands and the effort to support their products within the outlets while gathering and using information about their customers through research and database building. Their real problem is in trying to build a bridge to their customers while maintaining the retail efforts that get their products into the customers' hands.

The retailers involved can be expected to see the customer as theirs and to accept the support and resources as part of the exchange that ensures that the manufacturer's products are sold. The retailers have long seen themselves as the customers of the producers and are therefore wary of the interest shown in the retail customers. Are the manufacturers seeking to cut them out of the process by selling direct? Both parties are constantly trying to balance their needs and interests in this sort of relationship and the outcome is often one where people become customers to both parties – a situation that seems easier for the customer to accept than either of the other two parties!

Points of exchange

Retail may cause a dilemma for some, but the whole range of points where an organization can connect and exchange with its customers presents you with opportunities to support the emotional route, boost retail sales and thereby support your retail partners, develop relationships, and so on. Figure 3.6 provides a range of points of contact and means of exchange. The communications cover everything from the provision of basic information through to image building and the development of relationships. It is helpful to remember that if the communication is not private and one-to-one, its message may be received by people at different stages in the process (some considering purchase, others in the process of buying and those who have already bought).

	Pre-sales communications	Sales transaction	Post-sales
I N D I R E C T	Broadcast/narrowcast advertising Public relations Promotions– 　　Displays 　　Leaflets 　　Brochures Video/CD/DVD Web advertising including banners, flashes, pop ups, etc. Own web site	Via– wholesalers retailers agents franchises brochures/catalogues Receive goods from third party (as per this section)	As for pre-sales
D I R E C T	Direct mail Telemarketing Own sales force Own retail outlets Catalogue/brochure Web site	Via– Postal medium Own telesales Own sales force Own retail outlets Catalogue/club sales Online sales Receive goods directly via sources in this section	Follow up call/letter/e-mail/visit, etc. Customer satisfaction research Maintenance/servicing agreement or advice Complaint/problem handling Long-term accounts/payment related repair insurance/warranty new product offer regular related sales (e.g. refills, spares, etc.)

Figure 3.6
Points of contact and means of exchange with customers.

Even the points that appear to be single purpose can have broader uses. For example, delivery is not just placing the goods in the hands of the customer. The approach and care of the people delivering the goods, their manner, appearance, and their trustworthiness and commitment to doing a good job can have a powerful effect on customers (as can the opposite experience). The speed and timing of delivery work together with this, as does the way in which the goods are wrapped, labelled and documented. The person who orders well before an event such as Christmas but does not receive the goods until afterwards will be deeply unhappy with the service. If the delivery is slipshod, the goods badly packaged and the delivery staff surly there will be no room left for customer services to retrieve the situation. In such an example everyone loses as customer service staff learn to hate their job, delivery staff feel undervalued and the warehouse staff feel under siege.

ACTION BOX 3.6

For each of your organization's key products/services, list all of the organizations, agencies, media and individuals that are placed between your organization and their customers. Who controls and directs them? How could they be improved/assisted and could any be removed or replaced by an activity or part of your own organization?

Out of the various points of contact involved, the ones most likely to affect the customer's experience and attitude are also the least prestigious where cost cutting is most likely to be targeted.

GAPS AND OTHER OFFERINGS

We have seen the route to customers from both sides and have discovered that it is not simply a process or physical route. It is also an emotional path taken by the customer, supported and guided by you.

By spending time studying the routes you have, and comparing them with those of your competitors, it will become apparent that there are gaps in both processes and between needs and fulfilment. Nothing, it would seem, is perfect.

As part of your research and planning activity you should spend time trying to identify these gaps and deciding what they mean to you. Here are five possible types of gap to look for:

Opportunities missed

Are there things you can do to help shorten or improve the route to your customers? Are there things you are doing that your competitors do not do and could these be used to help you to differentiate (i.e. make them stand out in comparison with your competitors) your products or services? What good things were you not aware of and what good things are possible?

Traps

There may be good reasons why you do not do something. Perhaps it is more dangerous to overreach yourself? Perhaps it is inappropriate in the eyes of your customers? Check each potential opportunity for flaws and avoid creating problems for yourself.

Competitor tricks

What can you learn from your competitors' approaches? You all provide roughly the same thing so what do they do differently and what can you incorporate into your own process that will enhance it? Good practice and good ideas cannot be rejected simply because the opposition thought of it first.

Customer needs

Gaps pointed out by customers are often the ones that are most important. If you do not address their concerns someone else will – and reap the benefits, too. Customers are usually the richest source of new ideas, improvements and new applications of existing products or services. Some organizations ask customers after they have developed new products, other organizations have customer user groups where they provide customers with a forum where good ideas keep turning up.

Organizations also have needs

A large part of the route to customers, from your perspective, is made up by parts of your organization. What can you do to improve internal processes that will help shorten or enhance the route? Each action in this context has at least two complementary effects. It is directly beneficial to the organization and is also beneficial to the customer (therefore being even more beneficial to the organization). A third effect is that such improvements also benefit you.

ACTION BOX 3.7

Using columns headed 'Internal customers' and 'External customers', try to identify and list at least one gap for each of the types explained above. Use the notes, charts and tables you have already created to help you with this. Are there any other gaps that do not fit any of these categories? Write them down, too. Make notes on how you might deal with or make use of these gaps.

FOCUS ON INTERNAL MARKETS

Much of what has already been covered can apply to internal markets, often without much of a shift in emphasis. The translation can cause problems in areas such as communication, exchange and competition where you either do not recognize the process as being the same, or where the emphasis is different or elements are missing. An example of each might help you here.

Communication

Communication in the internal market may not seem anything like that experienced externally but a lot of important issues in this area affect both how you and your department serve internal customers, and how those customers form expectations, opinions and ultimately experience your work. Internal communications will include:

- Memos, letters, e-mails, reports and other written material.
- Forms, printouts and data sets.
- Telephone calls, inwards and out.
- Face-to-face interactions.
- Attitudes of staff.
- Appearance of staff and office spaces.
- Meetings and presentations run or contributed to.

The agreed style and appearance as well as attitude shape the image you and your department have within the organization and will determine expectations and, ultimately, the value placed on your department's output. This can be important in terms of details (spelling and grammar, layout, agreed 'house style') and in terms of how people experience your policy (always agree timing and details, never omit or delay, always keep customers well informed, etc.).

Exchange

Exchange in a commercial context involves price, costs, profits, and so on. Internally, these may not be so obvious but there will invariably be a cost involved where a department or individual fails to deliver or delivers badly or late. While the cost may not be easily measured or directly apportioned there are usually consequences. So, departments who fail to meet their internal customers' needs properly may end up costing the organization money whilst losing possible bonuses, being placed lower in the list for allocation of resources and becoming an unattractive place to work or recruit staff from. The opposite is often true when a department performs well and especially when it exceeds expectations. Good interdepartmental communications in these circumstances also may help.

The perceived and actual costs related to exchanges in the internal market can often be exaggerated by the lack of choice in suppliers (see below) and poor service associated with no alternative has always been a recipe for dissatisfaction. However, generally it is better to focus on the improved benefits possible from increased performance than it is to look at the cost of poor results.

Competition

Competition as an element of internal markets has already been discussed in earlier chapters. We often assume that structures within an organization are both logical and stable but this is not so. Reorganization means creating a new and different organization – and roles as well as jobs can change or disappear. If something is not working well or a new way of doing something is developed, organizations will change. So, competition can be with potential change as much as with other departments or suppliers.

Studies of organizations also show that there are incidences where functions shift from one department to another as a result of poor performance. One example is where a person or department is failing in a service chain. In such cases communications and other activities begin to leapfrog the failing department. Another example is where the cost of a service provided internally cannot be justified against the quality of the service.

It has also been shown that successful and dynamic departments will either grow and become more effective and powerful across a wider range of activities, or they will become more secure and powerful within their own area of work. They seldom stay unchanged for long.

ACTION BOX 3.8

Select two of your own internal suppliers and, as their customer, evaluate them under the headings above (Communication, Exchange and Competition). How well do they do and how does your brief analysis compare with your view prior to this exercise? What can you use both to help them improve their performance and improve your own, too?

THE BALANCING ACT

Managing the process of meeting customer needs requires that you balance the needs of internal customers with external ones, that you balance the needs of stakeholders with those of the organization and again with those customers and that you do this within the aims and objectives set for you and your colleagues in the organization's strategies and plans.

We have used this chapter to explore more of the physical and mental processes that determine how we see and serve our customers and how they see and are served by us. We will take this further in the following chapters, and to begin finding that balance let us look at how you can start to bring some of the details together.

Figure 3.7 is a summary of a market research department's internal customers and against each is a brief comment on what/how they are served. Alongside this is an assessment of each customer's level of importance and roughly how much time is spent serving each of them. There is a reasonable amount of overlap in the time column as work on any given project may serve more than one customer. Figure 3.8 then maps customers against importance and time spent on them.

Code	Customers	Comments	Importance levels[1]	Time spent[2]
A	Marketing dept	Source of most commissioned work	5	70
B	Board of company	Monthly summary reports required	3	15
C	Sales dept	*Ad hoc* analyses and projects	2	25
D	Accounts dept	Budgets, bills, mgmt info., etc.	1	5
E	Manufacturing	Reports, mainly via A and B	3	10
F	R & D	2 or 3 p.a., mostly market tests	3	10
G	External customers	Dept views research as being the customer's only voice in the company	5	70

[1] 1 = very low; 5 = very high   [2] Rough estimated percentages of total time

Figure 3.7
A market research department's assessment of internal customers.

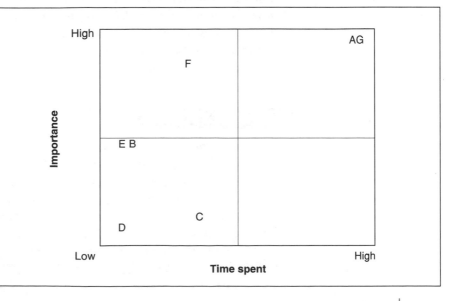

Figure 3.8
Mapping customers – by importance and the time spent on them.

This mapping exercise was then used to help the department discuss its priorities and apportion its efforts for the coming year. Being a research department they asked each of their internal customers to assess their importance against the other customers the department served. It revealed some interesting issues (see Figure 3.9). Whilst even the accounts department recognized that accounts was not a prime customer of the research department, each department had its own priorities. The biggest split was between the manufacturing and R&D departments, and the other departments. The level and type of support being given by one research department to the other was clearly not enough and there was a case that all other customers including the external ones and even the accounts department might benefit from improvements in that area. The improvements took place as a result of doing some analysis of what was important to them as a department and by listening to all of their customers as well.

Figure 3.9
Ranking
customers – by
their level of
importance to the
department.

Ranking	A	B	C	D	E	F
Most important	A	B	C	B	F	F
	B	A	A	A	E	E
	C	C	B	C	C	C
	F	E	E	E	A	B
	E	F	F	F	F	A
Least important	D	D	D	D	D	D

Question: *Thinking now of the role played by the research department and the relative needs of different departments for research services, rank the following departments by their order of importance, with the department that you think needs research services the most at the top. Where do you place your own department in this ranking?*

ACTION BOX 3.9

Use the balance exercise to evaluate your own department with regard to the other departments you serve and to external customers. Try to involve your staff in this exercise and listen to their comments and views carefully in order to represent the whole in the resulting table and chart. The example has abbreviated text but you can record as much as you think is important and relevant. Has it changed your own or your staff's view and, if so, how has it changed?

Competence self-assessment

1 Name the three most important things you and your department do for external customers, and why they are important. Which are the three most important departments to you and your department within your organization and how do they help you in your efforts to meet customer needs?

2 Choose a package holiday you have had or know well and try to map out the source and other people/companies involved in delivering the holiday package. Who was directly employed by the source company and what other types of relationship were there between suppliers and the source company? How did the source company control the delivery and quality of the holiday and where did they succeed/fail?

3 List the major inputs to your department – who in your department needs/uses them and how important are they to those individuals? Now do the same for outputs – who produces the outputs and which ones are most important to each individual? Describe your department based on these and compare it with your accepted view of your department.

4 Select a confectionery product and an insurance service you have bought and list their respective Core, Tangible and Augmented product attributes. How similar are they, where do they differ?

5 Review a purchase you made in the last year or so from the list of product/services below. Map your emotional route to, during and after purchase and assess communications and interactions related to this. Choose one from – automotive, white goods (cookers, washing machines, etc.), brown goods (stereos, videos, TVs, etc.), mortgage or other financial product, personal computer or similar.

6 List the advantages and disadvantages to selling a product through a retailer compared to selling it directly to customers.

7 Review your department's work within the organization and list its strengths and weaknesses in terms of communication, exchange and competition within the internal market. How can you take advantage of your greatest strength and address your biggest weakness?

8 Choose the two most important and the two least important internal customers your department serves. For each, write down a situation where you and your department would concentrate your efforts to serve that department to the

exclusion of all other work. Write down a situation where you would put each at the bottom of the priority list. How often have any of these situations actually happened? What does it tell you about the way in which you and your department serve the needs of internal customers?

CHAPTER 4

Competitors and how to make the most of them

External influences can have a major effect on organizations and their products/services. Competitor activity is set within this. A customer's market knowledge will be imperfect and may be based on experience of competitors and competitor activities. Communication is set within this context as is the route to improvements in delivery, image, service, communications, etc.

Why should we look closely at our competitors – this book is about meeting *our* customer needs?

The simple answer is that our competition may be trying to take our customers away from us and we may be trying to do the same to them. As a result of this, our customer's image of us will be affected by what they think of, and have experience of, our competitors as much as what they experience of us.

It is also important to learn from our competitors, as they may have noticed something about our customers that we have not yet noticed and they may have learned useful lessons that we can learn second hand. If an idea is worth using it should not matter where it came from and, indeed, many of those who think up good ideas end up not being able to take full advantage of them. As Tom Peters said, 'You can tell who the innovators are; they are the ones on the ground with footprints on their backs.' You should be making use of everything you can learn that will help you improve your relations with your customers.

Learning where you are positioned in relation to your competitors will also help you understand what your objectives should be and tell you what you have to do to make the biggest difference.

WHO ARE YOUR COMPETITORS?

Competitors exist within many different spheres. Some of you who have always operated on the principle that you were not in a competitive environment may find it disturbing to consider that competition exists for you, too. This chapter will help you understand the nature and scope of competition – whatever form it takes. In most cases this will exist within a market-place of some sort but it is a mistake to assume that markets apply to every situation. Where markets do not exist, understanding how provision is shared between organizations or agencies will help improve delivery to customers or clients. In a number of circumstances competitors will not be competing on the basis of shared or similar provision (see below).

What do we mean by competitors? Competitors are individuals, groups or organizations that provide alternatives to what you provide. They may offer these alternatives in a non-competing way and you may coordinate the provision with your competitors. If that is the case it will be easier to work with these providers to explore the differences between your provision, how the customers choose and how well you cover the spread of needs within your combined customer base. What you learn here is still important.

However, you may be in a situation of true competition where the alternative providers are seeking to win customers from you and you are seeking to do the same to them.

> Please note: *In some circumstances, notably in internal situations and in many bureaucracies, competitors will be competing to win resources, not customers. Departments and individuals who develop strong, customer-facing management practices will, as a by-product, strengthen their position within their organization. However, the competing for resources to the detriment of other departments within that organization is seldom the most constructive type of activity to pursue and usually deflects from the core purposes of the organization itself. As a result, this sort of competition will not be the focus of this chapter.*

We will begin our exploration of competition by identifying who our competition might be. So, starting with your organization, create a list of your key products or services and beside each one list the organizations that provide similar products or services. Based on your review so far of your department and how it operates and serves your organization, who would you say are your internal competitors? Who are your co-providers?

ACTION BOX 4.1

Put together the list of competitors as recommended above divided into internal and external competition. Try to rank your competitors from most to least important based on your current knowledge. Which criteria do you think are the most important to take into account when ranking them and why?

How many?

The number of competitors will reflect the area of activity your organization works in and will vary according to how specific or general your definitions are. For example, if you work in the travel industry you could have hundreds of competitors but once you define your market(s) you will reduce the numbers considerably. Other factors such as location and type of product/service will also refine your list. So, the competitors in the travel industry are too many to list, your organization specializes in holidays to Greece, and that reduces the list further. Once you take into account the price range, accommodation type and style of the packages themselves you will have whittled it down to a handful of direct competitors and a larger number of peripheral competitors.

Refining the initial list of competitors can then be carried out using the following criteria:

Are they direct or indirect competitors?

The closer their provision is to yours, the more direct they will be. Divide the group into direct and indirect, then grade them on their relevance to your organization by deciding how closely their products or services match your own.

How important are they?

Even if they provide directly comparable products or services, there may be other reasons why they are less or more important than other competitors. It is up to you to make that judgement. How important are they and why? It could be that a competitor is more important because of the distribution channel they have chosen or the regional nature of their operation and yours. Using the travel company example, if your organization sells exclusively in retail outlets you may not regard Internet-only providers as direct competition when there are two other companies with retail outlets close to your shops. Re-order your list of competitors according to their level of importance with the most important at the top.

The number of competitors you have will help shape how you respond to their challenges, but whether you have one or 100 competitors you will need to look at them in more detail.

Size and value

Size can change the whole perspective of an analysis. For example, you may only have one competitor but if it is 20 times larger than your organization it will be a significant competitor. Similarly, you may have a competitor that is, on paper, very large but the part of that organization competing with yours is very small and badly resourced so its current importance is not very great. Its potential threat may, however, be much greater.

You can measure size in a number of ways. The main factors are as follows but there may be other factors relating to your situation you feel are also important.

How many staff? Numbers of staff may be a significant element of the equation but numbers of people devoted to specific tasks may be even more important. So, they may have a very large sales team but few customer-support staff, or they may have a large proportion of their staff in a central HQ while your organization is more widely distributed. Defining *who* is important when involved in counting *how many*.

How many customers? The number of customers each competitor can claim as theirs will also set things in context. The number can be measured differently according to the circumstances. How many customers do you have compared to your competitors? If you operate nationally and your competitors are all regional how do you make the comparison? Is it relevant for you to look at it regionally? Again, choices make a difference and all relate to what you are trying to measure.

Total value? What is your market worth and what share of that do you have compared to your competitors? When you count relative values you begin to see things in a new light. Try this over a period of time, say five years, and work out how well your organization is really doing compared to its competitors. Another measure of value might be total profit rather than total sales. Looking at profit might change the order of importance of competitors or change your organization's position within the ranking.

Combined measures. Once you have gathered some basic facts and figures on your competitors you can begin to combine them to add new dimensions to your understanding. Combine value and customer and you can see what the average value a customer is to each organization, compare staff-to-customer ratios, or profit per customer. Adding a time or regional element can also change the view showing you who is improving their position, who seems to be in decline and where to find better returns for your efforts.

ACTION BOX 4.2

Using your list of competitors from Action Box 4.1 above, create a separate file for each competitor and compile information based on the seven criteria discussed above. Which sources have you used for this? Have you tried to see copies of a competing company's annual report? Have you asked particular departments within your organization? Are there trade figures or industry research data/reports that you can use? Begin to keep a separate file where you record all useful sources of information on competitors.

OVERLAPS AND CONFLICTS

Find out what you share with your competitors and you will learn a lot about yourself as well as how to improve your performance against the competition. We have already seen how location is a potentially important factor you might share with competitors. Time is another element revealing both how well you perform over time but also how time might provide space for improvements and developments balanced against the advantages of being new or being well established. Each aspect has its benefits and disadvantages. Here are some other aspects to explore.

ACTION BOX 4.3

The following section outlines a number of important types of information you should gather on your competition. Using the files you have already set up, record not only what you find out about each competitor under the headings but also where you found this information.

Customer bases

It is obvious from personal experience that customers are likely to use more than one supplier. Even the most loyal customer is likely to buy elsewhere from time to time. However, knowing the degree of customer overlap experienced between competitors will help you understand your market better.

There is only one way to find out about overlap and that is through research. If your organization has a database of its customers then it will be able to (and probably already does) carry out a very efficient and reliable survey or other data-gathering exercise on a regular basis (say annually) to help it measure the extent and types of overlap. With small customer bases it may be possible to keep regularly updated records using sales staff or other regular customer contact people. If your organization has no such opportunities, it may employ a research agency to help them find out.

A number of industry sectors produce joint research where all of the major players in the sector carry out co-funded research or they buy into a large piece of regular research carried out by a large market-research company. These research sources provide good market data and form the backbone of much follow-up research by individual companies.

The types of information most valuable to you will depend partly on your market or situation. In addition to the basics such as what proportion use other suppliers, how often, how committed are they to you versus your competitors, and so on, you may want to explore relative values of purchase, the circumstances when using different suppliers, and whether specific personnel or other factors are involved.

Demographic and other similar data will be closely linked to the behavioural information (as we saw in the last chapter) you gather in this research. So, you and a certain competitor may have very little overlap of customers but both be seeking the same types of customer.

The overlapping customers may help you find out what is going on here. Similarly, you may have a competitor whose core customer-base is quite different to your own but your overlap is completely biased to one or other market (either they are unexpectedly gaining your customers on a part-time basis or you are gaining theirs). Again, you will now have something important to investigate. Who your customers are and how they behave becomes much more informative when you can place them in the context of your competitors' as well as your own situation.

You may discover that some of your assumptions are destroyed by this exercise as you discover why customers choose to go elsewhere, or the extent of their commitment to you and other suppliers.

Products/services

A careful examination of what your competitors provide will always reveal unexpected information. Examination of this type should not be left to the technical group alone. It is surprising how poor competitor knowledge can be in some groups within a given company.

The questions you need to ask are: how is your function performed within competing companies, and how do each of the different elements that make up your competitor's product or service come together to make what they supply clearly theirs? At this stage you are not looking from the perspective of a customer but from a fellow supplier.

Start with the different physical or tangible aspects. How are they put together and thought of by the supplier and how does their approach differ to yours? Consider the aspects of your product or service you are most familiar with and seek them in your competitor's. How are they treated and apparently viewed when looked at from your competitor's position? Do the same with the elements of presentation they have put together – packaging, documentation, etc. Then look at their advertising and promotional materials and how they provide finance or other support at the point of purchase. How are they bringing their versions to the customer, and how are they backing it up with after-sales products and services?

If you have not spent some time looking at your competitor's approach, how can you expect to compete with them? This applies to accounts departments just as much as to customer service departments. Knowing something about their invoicing and credit handling might help you add extra value over competitors by doing something outside the experience or understanding of the marketing department but which directly affects your customer's experience.

Image

Image has three facets for consideration here.

First, it is worth comparing the projected image of your competitors against your own. Where there is ample advertising and marketing materials it is possible to carry out comparative analysis with your own image as the starting point. Where information is more limited you will need to resort to a range of competitor analysis and intelligence-gathering methods as described in Chapter 6. However, what you should look for is where the overlap lies between you and your competitors and where their images differ.

Second, what image is prominent in your customer's mind when they think of your organization and its products/services? How do they regard your competitors?

Third, how does this compare with your competitor's customers and their image of your organization compared to their favoured supplier?

The more you can find out about this the clearer your own image will be of your organization compared to others. You can then begin to address how to change and improve the image through promotion and marketing activities, and consider how this image is made up of other aspects of the customer's experience. You will then be better placed to change practices most likely to have a positive effect on image.

Customer service

Comparisons with competitors may not be welcome but they will be informative in this area, too. As well as telling you how your customers are treated by your competitors it will reveal both what your competitors think is important in this area and just how much they are willing to invest in it.

Therefore, it will not be enough to judge competitors on the extent of their work in this area. It is possible to discover that your competitor spends very little in this area and assume that you are doing better than them as a result. It may be true, but it may also be the case that their minimal investment focuses on the key area of support required by their customers, while your higher level of investment fails to meet your customer needs as effectively. A critical and open assessment is required here.

Quality, content

Learning from your competitors involves looking at your own products or services in the light of what you have learned from studying your competitor's work. Once you have dissected and analysed each aspect of what your competitors provide, you should look at the provision as a whole. Consider the quality of what they offer and the quality of the support and everything else that accompanies it. At each stage of your examination ask yourself how this compares with what your organization offers. Grade the quality as you consider each aspect and judge it against what you provide.

It is as important to understand why your organization does things better as knowing why your competitors do some things better than you. What do you need to support? What can you borrow from competitors? How are you going to make those changes?

Price

What will customers pay and what do they pay for the products/services you and your competitors offer?

We will spend time exploring this subject so we can concentrate on what we can learn about ourselves and our competitors from pricing.

There are four main aspects to consider at this stage.

Shared pricing

Is there little or no difference in prices within your market? This may not exempt you from competing on price. You have to consider what it means to be operating in a situation where price parity seems to exist. Each player within the market may offer different versions of the same product or service for a given price or price band and your presence in this market will define the status and quality of your organization compared to the whole market. Your closest competitors will be very similar to you and there may be little to distinguish you in the eyes of potential customers, so the strength of your identity and the perceived value of your offer will make all the difference.

A good example of this type of market would be the home computer market. Without studying it closely you would assume that the important basis of sales is price, but the market is strongly stratified with ranges of products in each and companies offering almost identical machines for almost identical prices. Add-ins and services begin to make the difference, and convenience, image and finance tip the scales in individual decisions to buy.

Price differentiation

Price can help to define where you and your competitors are within the market. Price in this situation is a definer of quality and customers at each level have either different levels of knowledge and expertise and/or have expectations. Again, the computer market shows how price stratification leads to price differentiation but there are many examples of this phenomenon.

Price sharing tends to show you who you are competing with, while differentiation may show you what your customers aspire to and are moving away from. So, price as an indicator helps you define the organizations you might wish to emulate in some way, or wish to avoid being compared to.

The hidden price

A number of markets have products or services where customers end up paying higher prices for their goods than advertised. Do you and your competitors have to deal with additional costs and have you ever considered what they mean in the context of the customer and competition? The new car has long played with this ingredient in its pricing. There are prices before negotiation, before trade-ins, before the added costs to put the car on the road, before additional optional extras, before tax and insurance and warranties. Then there are all-inclusive prices, prices including some of these extras as 'standard', and so on. How you and your competitors deal with these and use them to attract your part of the market can tell you both where you currently stand and what possibilities there might be in meeting customer needs while competing more effectively in the market-place. Research reveals that a surprisingly small number of people enjoy haggling or 'wheeler dealering' on price, yet some of these markets reward those who can haggle with better deals and lower prices. The source of dissatisfaction with car pricing in the UK is reflected in this and exacerbated by the equally unattractive option of buying overseas being made more frightening by the players in the UK market.

So, is part of the hidden price your customer has to pay an emotional one where they feel unhappy or uncomfortable and are likely to end up feeling dissatisfied even when they are treated well? How much has pricing got to do with issues of trust and the quality of information and customer support made available by you or your competitors?

Diminished price control

In some markets control of price becomes an important issue. In a number of retail situations the manufacturer has only a limited control of the price their goods are set at. If the retailer is prepared to accept very small margins as part of the pricing strategy they have adopted, or are even prepared to accept a loss on sales, this may affect how you and your competitors operate. If the discounting is not part of your organization's own strategy there may be a serious conflict. If the retailer controls a major part of the market you operate in you may find the retailer's strategy is an expensive way to compete that is difficult to opt out of. Conversely, your major competitor may be the beneficiary of the retailer's price-cutting strategy.

In some markets, the opposite can be the case, where suppliers dictate to a large degree what the price of their products can be sold at.

In both situations, how you and your competitors are placed and how each organization deals with it will tell you the status of customers in the relationship and the organization's priorities. What, for example, does it mean when a company vetoes all forms of discounting of their products? What sort of image can be built from regularly discounting a product? What effect does it have in positioning competing products or services?

Supplier/retailer relations

In a number of markets where a third party provides the outlet for an organization's products or services, the relationship between the two parties will be pivotal in the development of customer relations.

We have already explored one aspect of this where pricing and discounting can be important. Other important aspects in this relationship include:

Commission

In a number of these relationships the presence and use of commission is critical with products or services being given preference and being promoted by sales staff because of financial and other rewards being offered for sales. In these cases the effect on profit margins is a reduction passed on to the supplier with benefits to the retail/sales people and no direct benefit to the customer (except for the benefit of having your product/service which you regard as being superior). Just as there are price wars there have been commission wars with a variety of potential problems arising for all concerned. It can be dangerous if you and your competitors focus your competitive activities in this area as it can be a trap. How do your competitors approach this?

Training

A more customer-focused approach is where suppliers invest in the training and support of those employed to sell their products/services on their behalf. This always makes sense where there are new features, where technical knowledge is important and where there are legal requirements involved. In addition to ensuring that your product or service is well represented and properly sold, there are clear benefits to the customer in terms of quality of service and to the retail or sales people who gain professionally. Sales people will shape their image of you and your competitors based on this aspect of the relationship and you will learn a great deal about your competitors from their approach to training and support. It is also an area where retailers and sales organizations will tell you openly how your competitors operate and what they think of them.

Point of sale

Sales conducted in situations beyond your direct control create risks which can often be reduced through training (see above). However, there are frequently times when potential customers will be missed, where an untrained member of staff is encountered or where customers will encounter several options in the same outlet. Displays, stickers, leaflets, audio visual displays, and so on, will provide support to products or services independently of sales staff. Many of these point-of-sales items are welcomed and encouraged by retail or sales organizations. In addition to discovering more about your competitors while planning and placing these items, you will be able to monitor and evaluate competition through their point-of-sales materials.

Promotions

You will discover in later chapters how promotions can be used to support retail and third-party sales efforts as part of the strategy you adopt to drive your products or services through or along the supply chain. You can keep the third parties informed of your promotion plans, design promotional support into the strategy and show how they fit into the whole programme of promotions. While working with them in this area you will be able to discover how your competitors do this and what the retailers/sales people think of the different approaches. Just as you can develop relationships with customers that are designed to let them tell you how to develop your products and services, you can do the same with this group. Let them identify the best practices of your competitors that would improve your relationships with everyone along the supply chain.

ACTION BOX 4.4.

Take each of your competitors and identify the three key components, from the information you have gathered so far, where they are most similar and least similar to your own organization. Now compare this with what you understand to be the accepted basis upon which you and your competitors appear to be competing. Are they the same? If they are different, what does this tell you and how can you use this information?

BASIS OF COMPETITION

This chapter has explored competition in some detail but always with the customer in the picture. Let's bring together what you have learned under four headings.

Differentiation

If you do not know how your customers distinguish between you and your competitors it is difficult to know how you can either compete with them or improve what you are delivering to your customers.

This chapter has explored a variety of aspects of differentiation. It is up to you how you decide to develop those differences and use them to improve or change how you are seen by your current and potential customers. To evaluate what you have found out in order to be able to use it effectively, you will need to compare your current situation with those of your competitors and with your organization's aims and objectives. Listing and ranking these against different criteria will help your evaluation as will mapping you and your competitors against various differentiating criteria.

Share of voice

Competition can be measured in sales or transactions and these can be determined by the effectiveness of your communications. You have been exploring some of the ways in which you reach out and communicate with potential customers. Your success at this is measured not just by the total numbers of customers you reach and win. You share these communications opportunities with your competitors and much of your competitive activity takes place in this area.

Measuring share of voice can be a technical process where the total amount of advertising bought by each organization is measured in terms of the size and type of audience it reaches. The share of voice is then a comparison of the proportion of the total audience sought that each company reached with their advertising. As clever media buying could yield higher audiences for the same or less money, share of voice is different from a comparison of advertising spend. Comparisons by media types used can help you understand how you and your competitors see your markets and wish to be seen by them.

Research can also help you measure how prominent each of the competitors in a market is in the eyes of key consumer groups. So, in addition to advertising spend and share of voice per media you can look at the comparative effectiveness of your communications.

Customer retention

In later chapters we look at keeping, losing and winning new customers in some detail. Here, we will focus on customer retention.

Once you have won a customer, the primary objective behind meeting customer needs is to keep them as customers and develop a relationship with them in order to stop them from having a reason to seek alternative sources of what you offer. Regardless of what you or anybody else does there will always be a proportion of your customer base that will choose to buy elsewhere. The proportion of customers you manage to keep and the length of time you keep them will be measures of how good you are at meeting your customer needs.

Customer retention rates or their corollary, the attrition rate (the rate at which you lose customers), can be used as measures of each competitor's position in the market-place. If you can calculate an average rate of retention you can also compare your organization's performance against the market as a whole. However, if the retention rate is very poor generally, you need to ask yourself whether achieving a small improvement on it is enough to congratulate yourself. Markets with very poor retention rates are frequently vulnerable to new competitors with a fresh approach to areas such as customer care. It may indicate a more radical approach than anyone in your sector is prepared to take and therefore constitute a major opportunity.

Strengths and weaknesses

During this chapter you have been exploring the many facets of how you and your competitors operate. Bringing these different elements together will provide you with a very powerful picture of the competitive environment you operate in and where you are positioned within it.

An effective and informative method of summarizing this information is to list the strengths and weaknesses you have identified in your competitors and in your own organization or department. By comparing your position with those of each of your competitors you will be able to identify where each can be exploited to improve your own organization's position. Building on your strengths is obvious but we have also looked at how you can adopt and adapt your competitor's best points or strengths, and while addressing your own weaknesses you can exploit your competitor's. Chapter 5 looks at strengths and weaknesses in more detail.

ACTION BOX 4.5

First, assess each of your competitors against the six criteria in the section above and identify one key change your organization could make in each of the four areas that would improve their competitive position. What can you and your department do to contribute directly to each of these possible initiatives?

Competence self-assessment

1 What are the three main advantages you have over your key internal and external competitors?
2 Describe one improvement in each of the following areas that would increase your department's competitiveness – staff training, customer relations, value to customers.
3 What proportion of your organization's customers use your products/services exclusively? Can you show what could increase this percentage and what is stopping the increase?
4 How can pricing be used to help you improve your organization's competitiveness?
5 What can you learn from the way your competitors use communications? How would you apply those lessons to your current communications?
6 Identify and describe two important weaknesses in your current approach to competitors and explain how you could turn them into strengths.

REFERENCE

Peters, T. (1987) *Thriving on Chaos: Handbook for a Management Revolution*. London: Pan, p. 43.

CHAPTER 5

Starting the planning process — where do you want to be?

Establishing initial aims and objectives, defining the organization's aims
and objectives in the context of what has been learned to date, defining
the department's role in meeting the organization's requirements. An
important part of the planning process is being able to establish a
realistic and relevant shopping list. What are we planning for? Decide
where to aim before planning the route!

Most managers will not be writing the organization's or department's
first plan. You will have the organization's current or previous year's
plan containing what each department is expected to contribute to
the organization as a whole. In your departmental plans you will have
more detailed and specific information focusing on what you and
your staff need to do.

These plans do not appear from nowhere. They are the results of a
process where managers and staff develop the plans and discuss and
negotiate with others to produce an agreed formula for the way for-
ward. So, they are developed, agreed, accepted and acted on. The
structure of plans varies according to the organization, its situation,
its activities and the scope and timing of the plans themselves. They

can range from very basic action plans through to complex and comprehensively detailed documents.

Before you can begin to develop your own plans you will need to understand the scope and level of the plans you can prepare and how they fit into the organization as a whole. This is why the first part of this chapter looks at what plans are and how to understand them before it focuses on analysing the plans you already have access to that affect you. From your new perspective and understanding you can begin to put together a sensible shopping list of what you want to achieve through your own planning process. Later chapters will provide you with the tools to help you make things happen.

AN OVERVIEW OF PLANNING

Planning helps us to focus on the key tasks needed to ensure the highest levels of customer satisfaction. It ensures that we have assessed the risks and calculated the benefits of the actions we are taking.

What is planning, what are plans?

Planning is an important discipline which forces you to rationalize why you are taking certain actions. A plan is not an end in itself, but a blueprint for action. Some managers avoid planning because they believe they have more important day-to-day tasks to deal with, others strive to produce an attractive document which simply sits on a shelf and is never translated into action. Both approaches are wrong. Without effective planning, your day-to-day tasks will lack direction; they will simply be responses to circumstances. And without action, your plans are wasted.

A well-documented plan provides a guideline for other people. It details their responsibilities and shows what they should achieve and when. Just as important, a good plan summarizes the thinking and the conditions behind the plan. If any of those change, the plan can be revised. Above all, planning should help you to meet customer needs more effectively. It focuses the mind of every member of your team on the key tasks needed to improve customer satisfaction.

ACTION BOX 5.1

Make a copy of your department's or other most relevant and most current plan and use the section below to compare the expected structure and contents of a plan with your own. It is likely that there will be a number of differences. Make a note of these and try to find out why they are missing or why other details have been added. Decide which parts are due to 'house style', which are due to the specific nature of your organization/department, which are omitted due to assumed knowledge, etc., and which should be added.

Characteristics of a good plan

Good plans share a number of important characteristics:

- They address the relevant issues.
- They are focused on action and include an action plan.
- They are practical and achievable.
- They incorporate clearly defined objectives.
- They include strategies which can be implemented easily.
- They allocate responsibilities and identify expected results.
- They are measurable.
- They are flexible enough to accommodate change, failure and success.
- They are easily updated or revised.
- They include timings and costings.
- They include a summary of the background to the plan.

Structure of a plan

The formal structure of a plan is similar to a management report and includes most or all of the following elements:

- Introduction.
- Management overview.
- Background.
- Overview.
- Objectives.
- Strategy.
- Action plan.
- Budget.

- Evaluation procedure.
- Change control procedure.
- Contingency plans.
- Conclusion.
- Appendix and technical data.

Introduction   This is usually a brief statement of who produced the plan, for whom and why.

Management overview   This will be a précis of the key points of the plan. It is often presented as a series of bullet points and is unlikely to be more than a page long.

Background   The background describes the reasons for the plan and provides a context. It can include analyses, together with a summary of market and other external factors. A number of techniques for analysing these external factors are discussed later in the chapter.

Overview   Like the management overview, this section outlines the key points and conclusions of your plan. It can be an extended version of the management overview for colleagues who require a more detailed introduction.

Objectives   This section explains what the plan is designed to achieve. It relates the specific objectives of the plan to overall corporate objectives and indicates the priorities within the plan.

Strategy   Outlines the approach that will be adopted in order to meet the objectives. It usually includes timescales, costs and resource implications, together with the anticipated benefits in business and financial terms.

Action plan   A detailed plan for each stage of the strategy, allocating responsibilities, targets and timescales for each activity.

Budget   This section should show the total anticipated cost for the project, together with a cash flow forecast for each of the key stages.

Evaluation procedure   Plans should include key targets and deliverables that can be constantly monitored. This section should describe the review stages and the actions that would be taken if targets are not met.

Change control procedure   This section explains how any changes to the plan should be authorized and incorporated into the plan. It may include formal procedures for notifying other team members of the changes so that there is no possibility of confusion.

Contingency plans   These are plans designed to deal with specific circumstances that have already been identified. One approach people often adopt in this section is to include a series of 'What if...?' scenarios with appropriate responses.

Conclusion   This is a summary of the main conclusions of the plan, together with an indication of the expected results.

Appendix and technical data   In this section planners will include detailed information, analyses or technical data which may only be important to certain team members involved in the plan. In other words, the information is important but it may not be essential to everyone involved.

THE IMPORTANCE OF ACTION PLANS

The action plan is an important element of most people's plans. It ensures that people achieve the results aimed for. Expect action plans to include the following elements:

- Action to be taken.
- Start date.
- Completion date.
- Staff responsible.
- Methods.
- Resources required.
- Special needs.
- Impact.

This action plan can be issued as a separate document to the main plan and circulated to everyone involved in the project. It helps to build understanding and awareness and ensures that there are no misunderstandings.

There are a number of techniques for managing projects that can be used to control an action plan and keep it on track. The Gantt chart is probably the most commonly used one. Managers often use the Gantt chart to share the action plan with all of the staff while monitoring its progress. If you do not have a plan or action plan available to you it may be that much of the information is on such a chart. Figure 5.1 is an example of a Gantt chart.

- The vertical column on the left lists the main activities.
- Beside each activity is a series of horizontal bars against a scaled horizontal axis representing time.

95

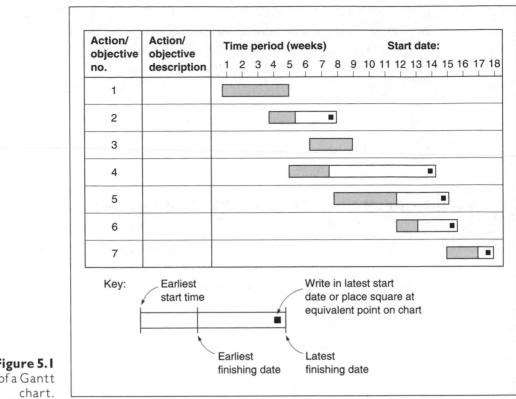

Figure 5.1
Example of a Gantt chart.

- The beginning of the bar is the start date for each activity and the end of the bar is the finish date.
- Shaded areas at each end of the bar can be used to indicate earliest possible or latest possible start and finish dates.

The Gantt chart is so popular because it is an exceptionally good yet simple tool for representing and controlling your project visually.

ACTION BOX 5.2

Select an action plan or project in your current departmental plans and use it to develop a Gantt chart which you can then use to implement the action or project. Once you feel comfortable with making a Gantt chart, select a project one of your staff is about to start and work with that person to make a chart for that project, too.

OBJECTIVES AND PRIORITIES

What are the objectives like in the plans you already have? How can we make sense of them and begin to do our own planning?

Objectives should be SMART:

- **S**pecific – Keep them clear, simple and to the point. Try to do one thing at a time.
- **M**easurable – Measure the costs and the outcomes. Exactly how much do you expect to increase things by?
- **A**chievable – Is it realistic, can it be done within the constraints?
- **R**elevant – Is it compatible with the department's and/or the organization's objectives/plans? Do you really need to do this?
- **T**ime-constrained – How long will it take, when will you start, when will you finish?

When it is time for you to set your own objectives they will have to fit the above criteria. Remember, there is no point in having objectives that you cannot achieve, that have no time limits, that you cannot measure in some tangible way or that do not fit in with the rest of what your organization is doing. This does not mean that objectives should be easy to achieve; they need to be clear, realistic and actionable.

You will also have to ask the following questions about the objectives in any current or recent plans for your organization and department:

- *Are the objectives customer focused?* How do they refer to customers? Which customers do they refer to? Are they addressing customer needs? What do they expect from, and what do they offer to, customers?
- *How do they impact on internal customers?* Are they part of the equation? Do they gain or lose? Will your relations with them be affected and, if so, how? Do they take what you or your department provide into account?
- *How do they impact on external customers?* Apply the same sort of questions as internal customers.

ACTION BOX 5.3

Take each of your department's objectives and test them against the SMART categories. What can you improve as a result?

MILESTONES AND MEASUREMENTS

Managers are responsible for ensuring that their staff carry out their responsibilities effectively. Monitoring progress enables them to spot any potential problems and take remedial action before the problem impacts on the success of the whole project.

Plans usually contain timings and expected outcomes based on the objectives and the action plans associated with them. There will be a set of measurements included in the plan that will be used to tell everyone whether they have met the objectives, exceeded them or failed. Usually a plan has a number of these at different stages and we sometimes call these milestones as they mark significant points along the path.

As well as monitoring progress, there will be other ways by which the managers involved in carrying out the plan will be able to review progress with the rest of the team. These may include managers doing some or all of the following:

- Plan to hold regular review meetings at key stages of the project.
- Plan to recognize team achievements such as early completion.
- Have contingency plans to provide support if team members encounter difficulties in meeting targets.
- Have plans to discuss actions to overcome problems and involve the team in any fundamental changes to the plan.

REVIEWING YOUR CURRENT PLANS

Once you know what to expect from the plans in general you can approach them in a way then helps you focus on the issues of importance to you at this stage. You will be aiming to review those current plans to assess their level of customer awareness and their responsiveness to customer needs. Your initial focus will be on the stated aims and objectives of the plans. How customer focused are they, which parts are truly customer focused and what could be improved or developed from them?

By reviewing strategies and looking more closely at the action plans you will be able to assess their customer focus in more detail. So, which elements and actions have a customer focus and which fall short of the mark? Which perform internal support roles and which would be improved with more customer focus? Finally, how do these plans impact on the internal and external customer chains and how can these be improved or focused on better?

Current aims and objectives

To help you make a reasonable assessment of the current situation you can draw up a simple table as illustrated in Figure 5.2. Against each aim and objective in your department's plan write down the principle recipients of benefits based on the aim or objective. Then, write down what you think each player is getting and, in the final column, a brief note on the resources/staff required to meet the aim/objective.

Aims/objectives	Principle recipients	Benefit to recipients	Summary of resources required

Figure 5.2
Example of an aims/objectives review form.

At a glance you will be able to see who the plan appears to be aimed at serving and you will be able to compare your interpretation of the plan against the table. How does it differ and why? Possibly there are *activities* carried out by your department that are *not covered in the plan*, or only referred to but not part of the written document. You will need to think carefully about what this means.

There may also be *gaps that are obvious* now that you have begun to explore the relationships that exist between you, your internal customers and the ways in which the organization serves external customers.

Finally, listing all of the objectives does not measure the comparative importance of each against the others. You may have six objectives, of which only one has any strong relevance to the customer. However, that might be the key objective and hold precedence over all others. So, you need to consider how each aim and objective relates to the others and *how important they are in the total picture.*

FITTING INTO YOUR ORGANIZATION

The sort of organization you work for will help to determine the sorts of plans you have and the roles you are expected to play in them. Much research has been done into how organizations are structured. Here are some basic types of organization and notes to help you decide what your situation is. Structural types include:

Simple structures

Small businesses are the most common version with one person running it and a group of people working under her/his direct control. How big such a structure can grow depends on what the organization is doing and whether it is run by a single person or a partnership. Growth will inevitably result in some major changes in structure. There is likely to be one plan for such an organization. Individuals within this type of organization may work together and have a shared plan or there may be one controlled by the owner.

Functional structures

Here, the organization is divided into the primary tasks being carried out by the organization (e.g. production, finance, marketing, etc.). Small to medium sized companies are like this and so are some multidivisional organizations where the divisions are semi-autonomous and have their own versions of the separate functions. Plans in such organizations can encompass the whole organization with departmental sections, or can be a set of departmental plans with a unifying strategic and operational plan.

Multidivisional structure

This is usually where an organization has divisions responsible for defined markets, products or services but it can be vertically integrated with divisions devoted to production or distribution as well as by region, product or service type. It is possible to be a manager with your own responsibilities and plans which fit together with other managers within the division, and where only the most senior people in the division have any detailed understanding of how the division fits together with other divisions and with the organization as a whole.

Holding company structure

In this context there are strong similarities between certain multi-divisional structures and this structure. Here we have a parent or holding company and a range of companies wholly or mainly owned by it who operate, to a varying degree, as separate companies. Unlike the previous type, each company runs a higher risk, is provided with less support and works less closely with its sister companies (or not at all). Plans in this structure are further from the central holding company when seen by managers in individual companies.

Matrix structure

This can be in large organizations where, for example, a multinational has trading companies which each operate in discrete geographical regions (Asia, Europe, USA, etc.) and where product divisions operate to supply their products across the regions. There are many examples from smaller organizations. A good example is in educational establishments where management is divided by subject, with heads of each subject running their areas providing teaching across different levels of the college or school (lower, middle and upper school head, for example). A number of different professional organizations structure themselves in this manner, too. Plans in such organizations tend to be developed in consultation with a number of different managers.

Multinational structures

These can vary and be any of the larger models but they tend to have a perspective which is both local and multinational. Your position within the organization and the role or function of that part will determine how local or multinational your perspective is. The plans you encounter in these organizations will vary for the same reasons.

Intermediate structures

The dividing line between different structures is not only grey, it can be confused by organizations in transition and by organizations making partial changes resulting in structures that are useful to them and their situation but hard to classify. The important issue is to look at your organization and decide how its structure is developing. For example, it may be too disruptive and complex for an organization to move from a functional to a divisional structure and resistance within the existing structure may also be a problem. Some organizations leave the problems until they become critical and then are forced to deal with the difficult and disruptive changes. Others become hybrids of the two structures and gradually move from one to the other.

Other forces can cause organizations to become intermediate in structure. For example, when companies diversify or take over businesses in other sectors or locations, they may retain their original functional structure while they have subsidiary companies employing other structures. Eventually the organization may change to absorb these subsidiaries or they may disaggregate or in some other way change. Multinationals often face these sorts of problems and may be able to take advantage of multiple locations to adapt and restructure.

Influences on these structures

A number of different things can influence the structure of your organization. These include:

Strategy

The strategic approach adopted by or imposed on the organization will shape it. Strategies can be based on financial or cost considerations, the type or limitations of the product or service range, how the market is developing, whether the organization is expanding or rationalizing, and so on.

Technology

This can range from the mass production organization through specialist processes to high technology or new technology, specialist or complex technology, various forms of research and development, high quality, low technology, and so on. Each will determine the pattern of the organization and the way in which it develops its structure. Your position within the organization will also be determined by the type of technology driving it.

Type

Is the organization large or small, is it public or private, how is it accountable to its owners or shareholders, etc? Is it aggressively expanding, powerful and static, or in decline? The type of organization it is will help determine its structure.

Environment

Does it operate within a simple or stable environment or is it in a dynamic situation? Is it a complex or a competitive environment? How hostile is the environment and can it operate beyond national constraints taking advantage of its multinational situation? Each will shape the way the organization responds to the environment and result in its particular structure.

The plans you have to develop and use will be responses to the structures and situations outlined above.

ACTION BOX 5.4

How can you define the structure of your own organization using the notes above? How does your department fit into this structure and can you draw a diagram mapping this relationship? How can you use this information to help you when dealing with your plans?

CURRENT KNOWLEDGE

You have already had the opportunity to consider what your department does and how it relates to internal and external customers. Now you have the opportunity to look at this and relate it to your department's plans. With three columns this time, you can list the *main activities* of your department, which *aims and objectives* they relate to along with how they are related, and in the third column you can *assess* how well you are currently carrying out this activity (including how customer focused they are or should be).

Again, the important thing is to cover all that you can in the first column and then do your best to ask the questions and answer them honestly. You are the judge at this stage and you can make the difference necessary to improve matters only if you know what needs improving and how to make the changes. Later you will have plans where the monitoring, measuring and assessment are an integral part of the process.

From this overview of current plans and what you are actually doing you can begin to compile a list of what you feel is missing, what you want to improve and the good things you want to keep and possibly develop. The following structure should help you to do this effectively. This is where details can matter; you can look at the small things as well as the large ones, you can consider what you want as well as what you need. You are going to compile what we call a shopping list. If it turns out that some things are not available, are too expensive or are simply unnecessary that does not matter. If you do not list them you may not find out, and if you do list them you may discover that they are more important than you realized!

Looking in

You should now have a good idea of the topics to consider when looking inwards into your organization. Here are some notes to help you:

- *You and your department* Your situation will determine the priorities you must have and will determine how much influence you have on the key areas that you identified in the work you carried out in earlier chapters. Every objective you have should be grounded in your department's and your own role within the organization. What do you and your department need, and what do you want to achieve?
- *Internal customers* With a clearer perspective, how can you develop your relationships with internal customers and how can you improve delivery of products or services to them? You need to identify priorities based on the benefits accruing to you and your customers.
- *Stakeholders* What specific aspects of the organization's activities are your stakeholders specifically concerned with and how can you influence the way in which these are managed?
- *Routes to customers* What are your inputs into the systems and what do you initiate and complete as part of the process? How are you a contributor to the adding of value through the process?
- *Barriers* What contribution do you make to reducing these barriers and where are you a barrier?
- *The competition* What can you do about them from your situation, what can you learn from them that can be used

by you or other players, how can you turn competition into cooperation?

Looking out

Although some of the same areas might be considered in this list, the focus outwards might change what you want to see happen, or change the approach or methods you want to list:

- *External customers* Know the sequence of cause and effect that means your actions will affect external customers. Where can your support and actions within the organization be better focused to improve external customer relations?
- *External stakeholders* The quality of your organization's activities will affect this group directly so what can you do to improve and develop these activities?
- *Customer interfaces* Is it your action or the information you select to use and distribute that will have an effect in this area? Even without direct access, your decisions may affect the way others handle customer interactions.
- *Barriers* There are a number of roles for barriers and some can be positive as well as negative. Can you turn even the most problematic barrier into a positive aspect of the organization's activities?
- *Competition* Creative approaches may bring unexpected results but basic information, basic logic and simple approaches need to form the core of your planned reaction to competition and competitor activities.

ACTION BOX 5.5

Choose one internal and one external aspect of your current plan and identify what needs to be improved/developed and what is good that can be built on based on your analysis. How will these affect other aspects of the plan?

Customer focus review

When you consider everything you have been looking at to date are there any general judgements you can make about how you, your department and your organization approaches customers? Along with your assessments at each stage there have to be more general things you need to express and review.

Here are the key questions you should ask about you, your department, other key departments linked to yours, the departments interfacing with customers and the organization as a whole.

- Generally, how focused are you/they?
- What is stopping you/them from doing better?
- What needs to improve? Is it knowledge, attitude, resources, support, direction, rewards, or what?
- How important is it?

Gaps and opportunities

You have been looking for gaps. In your review of your situation, as well as current plans we have looked at where there might be gaps and opportunities. Any shopping list of this sort would be incomplete without these. Bring together what you have discovered other people doing that you should or could be doing, including the things nobody is currently doing but which seem to you to be important or potentially useful, and also those things everyone claims are part of their plans or actions but seldom ever happen.

By definition, gaps are places where something is missing and opportunities are more than just possibilities. They contain advantages not yet taken. Once collected, each can be assessed.

THE NEW SHOPPING LIST

Perhaps shopping lists of this sort need to have a sign on the front of them saying 'Don't panic'. They always seem frighteningly long and potentially overwhelming. To reassure you it is important to realize that a long list is a healthy sign both for you and your organization. There is no such thing as a perfect organization and people who believe they or their organization does not need to improve are either irresponsible, untruthful or simply not very bright. So, congratulations on the length of your list. Now you can begin to assess your situation properly and begin to prioritize the contents of your list.

We have a set of questions that can be scored. They are the core of a bank of questions you will be able to use, adapt and revisit as you progress through the book. Each question has an answer that can be scored on a scale from one to ten. The lower the score the better the result. Look carefully at how we have set up the questions and the scale before you assign each a score so that you do not give an item on your list the wrong score. As you progress through the book you will discover that rankings and scores given here might change as your knowledge and perspective change. Again, this is not a problem – knowledge changes most things.

Taking time on this now will help you throughout the rest of the book so do not worry – you are not wasting time. As you ask the questions you may also find that your previous scores for other items on the list need to be changed. Please make the changes as they occur. At the end, you will discover that you now have the tools to begin prioritizing what you do. However, this is not the final list, so, remember that we will revisit and revise parts of your list as we progress through the book.

You do not have to carry out this assessment in one sitting. Take sections and do them in between other tasks, and if you can do the work on a spreadsheet further changes and analyses will be made easier. Finally, you may find that some of the questions are not relevant. Do not try to answer irrelevant questions; this is a fairly broad bank of questions designed to give you a good range to work with. The key is to use the list, do not let it use you.

If you use a spreadsheet to record your responses, number each of the questions from 1 to 16 or A to P. Then, with the first column as the items on the shopping list, you can use the next 16 columns for the scores from the questions. You can then rank the list by scores for

Questions	Score and range of responses 1 2 3 4 5 6 7 8 9 10
How easy is it to achieve?	V. easy V. difficult
What proportion of customers will it affect?	High Low
How popular will it be with your staff?	V. popular V. unpopular
How popular will it be with your boss?	V. popular V. unpopular
How expensive will it be to achieve?	Cheap V. expensive
Will it save any money?	Lots None
Will it make/improve profits?	Lots None
Will it improve efficiency?	Lots None
Does it replace less-effective activities?	Lots None
What priority does it have (your view)?	High Low
What extra resources does it require?	None Lots
What level of technology does it require?	None Lots
How long will it take to achieve?	Short time Long time
What level of cooperation does it require?	None Lots
How close to your department's plans?	V. close Not related
How close to your key responsibilities?	V. close Not related

Figure 5.3
Bank of assessment questions.

individual questions or by their average score across all questions asked. The lower-scored items will be those that are better across a range of questions and may be the ones you want to put at the top of your list. If some of your key items have high scores you will need to ask why this is so. Is there a key aspect missing from the assessment or is it important regardless of its cost, popularity or ease of use, etc?

ACTION BOX 5.6

Apply the approach above to your own situation and keep a record of your work in your action book for future use.

Conclusions

Planning is a continuous process. Even as you are doing what you have planned there will be opportunities to develop your approach further. Continuous review and a desire to improve and develop are the key to successful management. However, you need to use the plan to keep you on course. Improvements need to lie within the scope and objectives of your planned actions, and diversions from this can dilute your effectiveness and even misdirect your efforts causing you to lose your way. Aim to keep a sensible balance between focus and openness in all your activities as a manager.

Competence self-assessment

1 Name the 11 key characteristics of a good plan.
2 List the 12 main parts used in a standard format plan.
3 Identify what you expect to be doing at work in the next week and draw a Gantt chart plotting all of your activities for that week.
4 Identify the milestones you will face for the coming week and explain how you will measure or evaluate them.
5 Describe the structure of your major competitor and explain how this affects the way it operates as a competitor in your shared field of activity.
6 Rank your department's tasks for tomorrow (or your next working day) in the order of their value to customers. Write a list of what you and your staff could do to improve the day's tasks in the context of your customers.

CHAPTER 6

Marketing — the tools for understanding and analysing

What else can we bring into the process in order to use the knowledge we have and start to develop processes to make things happen? Marketing provides us with useful frameworks, models and tools for analysing and explaining. Build the formal process that can be understood and shared internally, and that will fit with other departments and the whole organization while ensuring effective use of resources.

LISTENING, ASKING, UNDERSTANDING AND SHARING

Meeting customer needs should always be driven by what customers are telling you. We need to learn how to listen to customers. We also need to learn how to ask questions which includes choosing the right questions to ask and knowing how to ask them. Finally we need to learn how to make sense of what's being said to you by your customers, your colleagues and the market place as a whole. Asking questions, listening to people, and analysis, are key management skills, so what you learn in this area will help you in other aspects of your role as a manager. The route to these skills in this context is through a closer look at different aspects of research.

Listening

Researchers use a wide range of data from different types of sources. Some of the information they work with has been collected by them, or acquired through research they have commissioned, and some is from more general sources and may not have been collected for use by marketing researchers. The first sort of information is often called *primary data* and the other sort is known as *secondary data*.

In Figure 6.1 we have summarized the main types and sources used by researchers and marketers. We will need to explore these as we learn to listen to and respond to our customers' needs.

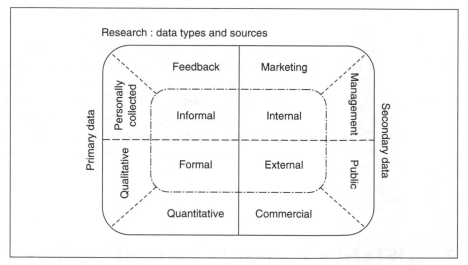

Figure 6.1
Research: data
types and sources.

Research should be relevant, usable, reliable and cost effective. Research has to inform but if it informs without meeting the first three principles its value will be questionable. So whether you are planning to carry out your own research or are sifting through existing information you need to move beyond the fact that the information is interesting and ask, 'Is this relevant, can I trust it and can I use it?'

Primary data

We can gather primary data in a number of ways. Figure 6.1 shows that we can obtain primary data from both *informal* and *formal sources*. *Formal sources* can be split into two types: *qualitative* and *quantitative research*.

■ *Quantitative research* concerns itself with measuring and is concerned with quantifying markets, opinions, attitudes, behaviour, and so on. The numbers of respondents tend to be quite large in order to be able to measure differences and ensure that the information is representative of whole groups or populations of people. The samples of people used have to be selected and measured across a number of criteria and the information provided is often used to make quantifiable decisions such as where to site a store, what the range of products should be or what price you can charge. It is usually carried out by specialist companies called research agencies as most organizations do not have the resources to carry out their own research.

Types of quantitative research you will encounter include all sample surveys using representative samples of populations. These will include surveys using telephone, face-to-face interviews, postal surveys, e-mail/Web/TV based surveys, other self-completion questionnaires, most hall tests, diary and similar surveys, all surveys where responses are measured and can be related to specific or measured populations and so on.

■ *Qualitative research* does not attempt to measure statistically. It is used to provide insights, add depth to existing knowledge, explore complex issues concerning organizations, their image, their customer's attitude, and so on. Often quantitative research is illuminated by qualitative research by interviewing a small number of people who can explain in greater depth why apparently contradictory answers have been given in a questionnaire or who can explain where attitudes or reactions come from. Conversely, qualitative research can be used to point research in the right direction, ensuring that the right questions are asked or that they are asked in the most useful way. Qualitative research can provide detailed understanding, providing some of the answers to the question 'why?' but it cannot tell you the answer to 'how many?' or 'by how much?' or 'by whom?'

This form of research includes elements from quantitative research where open-ended questions are not measured but used to illustrate or enhance data, but mainly it is research including group discussions or focus groups, depth interviews, workshop and most observational research and some forms of more informal research work.

Informal sources are less attractive to researchers and are often dismissed as hearsay. However, information from these sources provides managers with starting points, can signal potential problems and can enhance understanding while keeping you closer to your customers than you would otherwise be. Unstructured and *ad hoc* information cannot be assumed to be representative or reliable and the most common decision made as a result of this sort of data is a decision to carry out formal research to find out more. Also, informal feedback sources, if they prove to be useful, will be developed into more formal sources. The two subdivisions in Figure 6.1 can provide valuable information to managers aiming to meet their customer's needs.

- *Personally collected information* includes what Tom Peters describes as 'marketing by walking around'. The idea is to include a period of time in your working day or week which you devote to spending time to listening to your customers and looking at your interaction with customers from their point of view.

  Good examples of this include the department-store director or restaurant owner who spend time walking around their place of business listening to and watching how their customers are served. Another good example was set by the newer telephone banking businesses who insisted that their directors spend at least a morning a month sitting in on the telephone pool listening to and talking with their customers.

  The point of this activity is not to create your own measures of opinion or quality of service but rather to ensure that you have not lost touch with the business you are in. It brings to life the information presented to you as a manager and ensures that you keep asking relevant and useful questions. It may also highlight potential problems that may not be so obvious to those who are close to delivery all the time.

- *Feedback*. Although there will (or should) be formal and structured feedback systems in place, it is useful to develop and listen to more informal sources, too. For example, if your sales force complete regular feedback forms giving details on their customers do you still spend time with your sales people talking to them about their customers, the problems they encounter, the issues not covered by the forms, and so on? Of course you do! This process is part of the informal feedback identified here.

The relationships you develop with your customers and with those key people involved in serving your customers also adds useful information to your armoury which will ensure you perform well. Developing this further by starting a user group or a regular meeting where you bring together key customers for a social gathering of some kind may enable you to develop that feedback process and involve other key members of staff in the process. For organizations with large numbers of customers it may make more sense to have customer hotlines and other routes to help your customers give you feedback. The Internet can be used effectively in this process and many organizations have areas where customers post their comments, where frequently asked questions are answered and where direct questions and comments can be sent to named people or departments.

The important issue here is that all feedback opportunities given to customers must be properly maintained and supported and that the managers need to spend time doing the listening, reading the comments and experiencing what the customers experience. Benefits can include improved services, new product developments, increased customer satisfaction and the prevention of minor and even major disasters.

Secondary data

There are huge numbers of potential sources of secondary data and their uses are as varied as their sources. We can subdivide them in different ways, too, but here we will split them into *internal* and *external* sources and then subdivide *internal* into *marketing* and *general management* while *external* will be split into *commercial* and *public*. The research approach used to collect secondary data has traditionally been called *desk research*. It refers to the process of collecting, sorting, analysing and reporting on data published in reports, publications, and so on. This work has expanded as technology has changed and sources now include CD and DVD, audio, video and on-line sources including the full range of possibilities presented by the World Wide Web. Researchers are still based at a desk but their range of sources has been increased considerably and so has the speed of access.

Internal sources provide vital information that only your organization can collect and provide.

- *Marketing information* will include sales data and feedback from sales people, customer care and a whole range of other information gathered during the marketing process. Direct feedback from customers should include both the positive and the negative, with customer complaints and product or service failures and feedback from customer or client-user groups and other linked sources. All forms of marketing communication where responses are recorded or where there are feedback forms or database linked activities should also come under this heading as will data from websites, e-mail, postal and telephone traffic. The source is potentially extremely rich but depends on decisions to monitor, record and analyse the data available. Competitor data may also be included here although some will also be found below.
- *General management information sources* include all of the other data sources that may be found in your organization. Many organizations have a management information system which includes accounts, reports on press monitoring, general business reports, annual reports and a wide range of internal information on the organization, its people, clients, suppliers, competitors, and so on.

Until recently it was a simple matter to separate external sources into commercial and public sources. However, the Internet has changed the nature of information in both subtle and blatant ways which make this distinction much harder to make. In addition to most public sources of information (and many commercial sources) now publishing data on the Internet, it is possible to find a wide range of sources on virtually any subject if you search the Internet thoroughly. Unfortunately, not all sources are reliable, some are misleading or publish data they should not publish (for example, data they do not own or are using without the owner's permission) and some are simply wrong. Almost free access to endless sources of data does not make the researcher's job redundant. It makes training and experience essential.

■ *Commercial sources* include all sources provided or produced by commercial organizations. In addition to the research agencies and data gatherers who carry out their own surveys and analyses, there are a wide range of database marketing companies, press and information agencies and a variety of information providers and brokers who produce reports, analyses and on-line information systems. Many banks and other financial institutes produce information, too, and most commercial organizations produce information about themselves which includes useful data. Agencies produce regular research and data sets (such as directories) aimed at specific sectors, and groups of companies in different sectors, commission and publish sector-wide research and reports.

■ *Public sources* include a number of government sources that present themselves as the definitive data suppliers in particular areas (the National Census, the National Household Survey, and so on). Many such data sources provide difficult-to-use data in their standard reports and require both specialist knowledge and special access before they can be used for commercial purposes. However, the public sector does provide many vital benchmarks and a wide range of other data that are used commercially. Alongside the national agencies, regional and local authorities and bodies provide valuable information. Other public resources for desk research include information on companies (from Companies House) and information on imports and exports, etc.

ACTION BOX 6.1

Use Figure 6.1 to help you identify where your information about customers comes from. Draw the outline of the diagram and list within each box the sorts and amounts of information you can obtain about your customers from the category of source the box relates to. What types of information do you not have and where does most of your information come from? Is there a bias and is it a good one?

Asking

There are three components in the process of asking a question. The first component is *selecting* the right questions to ask, then we have to *specify* whom we are going to ask and then we need to decide how we are going to ask the question (*designing*).

Selecting the right question starts by deciding what your priorities are and identifying what you really need to know and understand. Begin by stripping your needs down to the most basic elements by listing them all and asking if you really need to know, when do you need to know, why you need to know, does some other source already provide you with the answer you need, can it be incorporated with something else, what will you do with the information, who else needs this, have they got the answer already, can you share the effort if they need it too?

By simplifying and then ranking the information you need you should be able to produce a shortlist of what appears to be essential. Test this list and its priorities with others involved; this may include members of your staff, your immediate line manager and colleagues working in the same area with you. Aim to produce a set of key topics or areas you need to investigate and against each outline your required outcomes. Do this in a short, two-columned table. From this you can develop questions covering the topics that will give you answers that meet your required outcomes. An example of this based on service provision in a local authority can be seen in Figure 6.2.

Topics of concern	Outcomes required
We have spent a lot of time and effort improving our Meals on Wheels service and invested a lot in telling people about it, yet we have not increased our customers' take-up of the service. What's going on? What have we done wrong?	Have we improved the wrong things or not improved them enough? Have we failed in our communications somewhere? What do we need to say or do to improve things?

Questions to ask
■ Please rank the following aspects of the Meals on Wheels service according to how important each is to you (1 = most important). Show list.
■ What other aspects not listed are important to you? Why do you say this?
■ Have you noticed any improvements to this service in the last three months? Please give details.
■ What improvements would encourage you to use this service?
■ Have you seen our advertisements for this service?
■ Did it encourage you to use/discourage you from using this service? Why?

Figure 6.2
Sample form.

The act of *specifying* may affect what you ask as it refines your thinking further. In the example above, the local authority began by assuming that they would use the staff who deliver the Meals on Wheels service to ask customers to complete a short questionnaire. By reviewing the topics, outcomes and questions, a flaw in their thinking soon became obvious. They also needed to ask those who were not using their service. Their focus moved away from the point of delivery to the other services currently providing support to groups who they believed would benefit from using the Meals on Wheels service. The change in thinking added an additional qualifying question to the list and changed the nature of some of the questions a little to take into account the fact that some people will not have used the service or not be familiar with it.

In consultation with the other service providers, they produced a questionnaire and a short information leaflet describing the Meals on Wheels service, who is eligible to receive it and how to obtain it. After answering the questions the respondent could then be given the leaflet. This was seen as an effective way of both listening and communicating at the same time and was seen by the other services as a way of providing an additional service to their clients at little extra cost to themselves. In order to ensure that the questions were asked of people who were eligible for the service it was necessary to provide each department with a clear set of guidelines specifying all those who were eligible. So as well as ensuring good targeting for the questionnaire and leaflet, the exercise improved interdepartmental communications. Because of the difficulties involved in trying to obtain a properly structured sample of the target groups (mainly due to lack of information and problems of access) and because of the benefits in reaching as many of the target group as possible, it was decided to cover as much of the target group as possible. Once they knew how to improve their communications they would be able to reach the rest of their target group.

Target sample specification

All those living within the Local Authority's area who are eligible for the Meals on Wheels service and can be reached through existing support services.

Questions

- Thinking of the Meals on Wheels service, have you in the past used/do you currently use/would you consider using this service? Please state why.
- Please rank the following aspects of the Meals on Wheels service according to how important you feel each is to you (1 = most important). Show list.
- What other aspects not listed are important to you? Why do you say this?
- Have you heard of or noticed any improvements to this service in the past three months? Please give details.
- What improvements to this service would encourage you to use/continue to use this service?
- Have you seen our advertisements for this service? Where was this?
- Did it encourage you to use/discourage you from using this service. Why?

Figure 6.3
Specifying stage.

The *designing* stage began by making sure the questionnaire and leaflet were simple, easy to use and performed their functions properly. The questions were tested in one 'friendly' department and improvements were made to the layout and some of the wording of the questions. The leaflet was also improved during this testing phase.

The team worked together with each department to calculate the total number of questionnaires and leaflets that were needed for the exercise and agreed the timing and procedures with each department. This helped to avoid failure through poor cooperation or poor administration. It was agreed that leaflets on the service would continue to be provided after the period of the questionnaire. Timing and procedures for collecting and returning completed questionnaires were tested and then agreed with all departments.

The team also agreed a report process as part of the design of the exercise. Basic results from the survey would be sent to each department so that they would know what the outcome of their efforts had been, and information on improvements based on the survey would also be shared with other departments. Of course, the results themselves would need to be presented to the key members of the team, and actions based on them discussed and agreed.

Of all the useful and important information gathered by the survey two main lessons were learned.

First, they found out what they had done wrong when launching their newly improved service. The images on their posters and in their other literature featured old people receiving Meals on Wheels services. They already provided a successful service to the vast majority of that needy group and the advertising could not increase this much further. However, all of the other target groups (housebound disabled people of all ages) predominantly understood that the service was for old people and not for them! A change in images and some text greatly improved their coverage of other groups.

Second, improved cooperation with and distribution of information through allied services changed the image and nature of the Meals on Wheels service and proved to be more effective in reaching key needy groups.

ACTION BOX 6.2

Identify one problem you currently face while serving an internal customer. Use the 'Asking' section to help you design a short questionnaire and use it to find out more about the problem and how you can begin to solve it.

USING THE PROFESSIONALS –
THE COMMISSIONING PROCESS

Research can test ideas or products, monitor effects, progress or change and help solve a number of problems. Before committing yourself to carrying out research you need to:

■ Decide the importance of the data you seek – what are your priorities?

■ Decide if research will provide you with the sort of answers or data you need.

■ Decide on the level and importance of the information you need – do you need to employ a research agency?

■ Decide on how and where to invest in your research efforts.

Most organizations use market research companies to carry out their research. The quality of the research data they obtain through such companies is determined by the quality of the relationship with the supplier and by the quality of their work. The following notes could apply to any relationship where you have an outside supplier.

The first stage is to clarify your own needs and the issues surrounding them. Consider the following:

1 Who is the research for? Is it for you, your boss or someone else?

2 What is it for? Identify exactly what you are trying to find out and why you need the data.

3 Is it appropriate? Can you get the data elsewhere? Are you asking too much of the research? What do you need to do before you begin the research?

4 What about timing? How urgent is it and what other time factors might affect it?

5 What about budgets? Can you afford what you want? What can you afford?

6 How do you want the results produced? How do you plan to use the results effectively?

7. Carry out the 'Asking' exercise in the previous section. Now you have a clearer idea of what you really want.

Once you have sorted out these details you need to select a shortlist of candidate suppliers. Most organizations that buy research regularly have a list of preferred suppliers. The research department or researcher will help you select the best candidates. If you have no experience in this area, guidance from a professional can be obtained from the Market Research Society. Please remember, this is only an outline of the process and not the definitive guide.

Before writing the briefing document spend time with your candidate research companies to find out what they can do and how they work. This will help you put together the most meaningful and effective document – one they can all respond to. When you first meet each of your candidate companies make notes on the following to help you assess their suitability:

- Ensure that you can get people with sufficient experience and skill to work on your project.
- Identify a contact you relate to, you find easy to communicate with and feel you can trust.
- How helpful are they and do they treat you like a prized customer?
- Make notes on how they manage their side of the meeting, how they interact as a team and what they think is important.
- How do they react to the outline you present at the meeting, are they more concerned with the price than the content, etc?
- Note any questions they ask between initial contact and the submission of their proposal. This might tell you a lot about how they work.

Now you can write your research brief. This is a basic document containing:

- The context of the research including as much background information as you think is necessary to explain why you want the research.
- Information on who needs it.
- Clear details of what you want to find out and from whom.
- Desired outcomes, possibly including how you plan to use the results, how it might affect decisions, and so on.
- The sort of research approach you want them to take (the methodology – face-to-face interviews, telephone research, preferred sampling, etc.).

- The level of contact during the project (i.e. regular meetings or contact during the research, progress reports, informal debrief before final results are produced, and so on).
- How you want it analysed and reported.
- Timescales.
- Budget details – what you can or are prepared to spend. You should already have a good idea of what you can get for your money based on your initial enquiries.

When they submit their proposals check the following:

- How well does each proposal reflect your briefing document?
- How well do they reflect your views and concerns as expressed in the meeting as well as in the briefing document?
- Did the questions they asked you add anything useful to their proposals?
- Do they really understand what you want to achieve?
- Will their proposals meet your aims?
- What have they added, changed or missed out?
- Do the analyses and reporting proposals meet your requirements?
- Was the brief delivered on time?
- Was it well presented and written?
- Are the costings within your budget?
- Are there any potential hidden costs?
- Do you think that what they expect from you is reasonable and possible?

Take your time considering their proposals and use the views and advice of colleagues to assist you. The company you select needs to be formally contracted to carry out your project and final details regarding the timing and payment for the work need to be formally agreed. The frequency, type and number of contacts during the project, the people designated to do the work, keep you informed and report to you will also be finalized at this point. Make sure you are happy with these arrangements before you make any formal agreements. As the customer, your needs have to be met.

SENSE AND PRESENTABILITY

Making sense of data and of what people say about data are two areas of management that seem difficult for a lot of managers. However, if you want to meet your customers' needs properly, you will have to take steps to ensure that you can understand the information presented to you. You have the interests of your customers, your staff and your own future to consider. Here are some guidelines to help you make sense of data and how to share that sense with others.

Who?

The first questions to ask when you are presented with data start with the word 'who'.

Start with 'Who does this data come from?' This comes in two parts. We begin by asking what we know about the source of the data. Earlier in the chapter we looked at sources. Is this a reliable source of information or is it someone's presentation of information from a reliable source? What do you know about the quality and reliability of the source? Does the source have its own agenda? Think about these issues as you begin to review the data being presented. Every table of figures or graph in a report or presentation should have a little note telling you about the source of the information used.

Alongside the source of the information is the origin of the data itself. Who was asked, who answered the questions, who have they used as the source of information in this table, presentation or report? Take note of the characteristics of the sample. Does the sample (or the part of it used in the table) represent the people you want to hear from? National figures may not be indicative of the attitudes or behaviour within a region, for example, and all adults are unlikely to represent the views of the young or the old or women or men.

You do not have to be a statistician to know that the right sort of people were asked.

How many?

Start as simply as possible. Find out how many people were used as the source of this information. Was it the appropriate amount for the task? If the research was qualitative you should not be presented with statistics as the point of the research is not to count but to explain and explore. So, how big or small a sample – tens, hundreds, thousands? If it is a small number, are you looking at a subset of the total sample? Even if a table only shows percentages and does not show numbers of respondents in each cell or box there should be a total sample figure. This will tell you how many people the table refers to in total.

Your first check is to see how big the sample was. The simple rule is, the smaller the number of respondents the less accurate the results will be. One way to test this is by looking at the largest and smallest cells in the table and asking yourself whether you can trust the smaller cells if you do not trust the larger ones.

Beginning to make sense out of size

Of course, it may not be as easy as big versus small. Here is an example to explain what to do. In Figure 6.4 we have some data from a survey. If it was being presented to you as the manager of KattK and DoggD, what would you look at first?

	All adults (%)	Cat owners (%)	Dog owners (%)	Buy KattK (%)	Buy DoggD (%)
North	25	20	30	15	10
Central	35	30	30	25	10
South	40	50	40	60	80
Male	45	35	40	20	10
Female	55	65	60	80	90
Total	100	100	100	100	100
Sample	500	200	150	45	38

(Source : National Survey of 500 shoppers, 23 June 2002, carried out by XYZ research)

Figure 6.4
Survey example.

Do not start by looking at your product data. Look at the total sample size. Five hundred is not bad as a total sample. Next, what do you already know? From other reports, surveys and official statistics you can check to see how representative the sample is across the three regions and between male and female. The figures you already have may show that the split between dog and cat owners is also quite close. The figures seem reasonable, so the survey is all right so far.

Now look at your product figures.

Before looking at the details check the sample size. Forty-five people said they bought KattK and 38 bought DoggD. What is that compared with the figures you know? Forty-five out of 500 is only 9% and 38 is 7.6%. How close are these to the national average sales figures you already have? In this example the expected figures should be around 15% and 10% respectively, so the manager knew the survey had failed to find a representative sample of his customers.

Finally, if the figures tend to become less reliable as the sample size drops what does that tell us about the figures for our products? Fifteen per cent of 45 people who bought KattK is only seven respondents; 10% of 38 is four respondents. As the sample is divided into smaller segments, each segment becomes less accurate, so, even if you knew that the regional breakdown was similar to what you would expect, it does not help you much. At this level of sample size its accuracy is more a result of chance than anything.

If the simple rule is, 'the smaller the number of respondents the less accurate the figure', why did the manager bother commissioning this research in the first place? Figure 6.5 explains why they bothered. Even with the smaller than expected sample of buyers they were able

	All adults (%)	Cat owners (%)	Dog owners (%)	Buy KattK (%)	Buy DoggD (%)
Chicken	60	55	30	40	53
Fish	74	65	15	66	5
Rabbit	30	33	40	45	60
Pork	21	15	10	5	5
Duck	15	21	15	24	70
Lamb	25	30	10	8	3
Prawn	12	35	6	66	7
Vegetarian	28	22	6	29	3
Beef	15	12	25	8	5
Total	100	100	100	100	100
Sample	500	200	150	45	38

Figure 6.5
Survey example.

(Source : National Survey of 500 shoppers, 23 June 2002, carried out by XYZ research)

to find out which ingredients buyers and owners preferred. The research shows very strong biases for both pet owners and customers. From these figures they can compare known sales and test new ingredients that are already popular with current customers while attempting to attract new customers by focusing on certain ingredients. The very small figures may not hold any accuracy for measurement sake but they do indicate a significant lack of interest in particular ingredients by customers. Conversely, the large percentages for those where customers have shown an interest in an ingredient indicate a strong preference. Only a deep distrust of the survey itself would indicate that the figures were not worth pursuing.

Only a very rudimentary understanding of figures is required to carry out such an assessment. The rules are:

- Keep it simple.
- Do you trust the source?
- Check what you already know – does it fit?
- Look at the sample sizes – are there enough respondents to make the results trustworthy?
- Are the differences in the figures big enough to demonstrate strong preferences, feelings or patterns of behaviour?
- Can you make sense of it?
- Can you use it, does it tell you something you need to know?

ACTION BOX 6.4

Select a report you have used in the past which contains research data obtained from a number of sources. Test the tables and information presented in the report against the guidelines above. What additional information have you now been able to extract from the report?

STATISTICS, DUMB STATISTICS AND MISLEADING INTERPRETATIONS

Despite the famous saying parodied in this section's title, statistics do not lie. People simply misuse them or deliberately use them to misrepresent the facts. It is pointless for a manager to use statistics to lie or mislead. You must use every little bit of information you have at your disposal to help you manage better. Here are some tips to help you get the most out of your data while avoiding other people's mistakes.

Some basic statistics

Here is a table from an imaginary survey looking at newspaper readership.

Figure 6.6
Newspaper
readers' survey
results.

Total respondents

	All adults	Male	Female	Age over 50 yrs	Age 30 to 50 yrs	Age 15 to 29 yrs
Paper X	300	120	180	150	100	50
Paper Y	400	180	220	160	160	80
Paper Z	600	340	260	200	240	160
Total	1000	495	505	340	410	250

Looking at the numbers of respondents may not be enough to make sense of the data. You might look at the figures and assume some of the following. Because paper Z has the most readers in total they can make claims in every category on the table. It can claim to have more readers in each category than any other paper. Similarly paper Y can show it has more readers than paper X. Apart from paper Z, more women tend to read papers than men and the older people are, the more likely they are to read a paper.

We can quickly improve our understanding of the figures by looking at percentages. Figure 6.7 looks at the column percentages. That means it takes each of the figures in a column and we work out what they are as a percentage of the total for that column. So, of the 1000 people who took part in the survey, 600 read paper Z. To calculate the percentage you divide 600 by the total number divided by 100 (1000 divided by 100 which equals 10). Six hundred divided by 10 equals

Column percentages

	All adults (%)	Male (%)	Female (%)	Age over 50 yrs (%)	Age 30 to 50 yrs (%)	Age 15 to 29 yrs (%)
Paper X	30	24	36	44	24	20
Paper Y	40	36	44	47	39	32
Paper Z	60	69	51	59	59	64
Total	100	100	100	100	100	100

Figure 6.7
Survey results –
version two.

60 which means that 60% (60 in every 100 people) claimed that they read paper Z.

Quickly, we see that the survey shows some people read more than one paper (the column percentages add up to more than 100) – something that is not so obvious when you look at the numbers of respondents.

Next, we can use the percentages to make some comparisons. For example, while 30% of the total population read paper X, 44% of people over 50 read that paper. To give yourself a measure of just how big that bias is, divide the 44 by 30 and then multiply by 100. The result, 147, is simply another percentage which measures the difference between all adults and the 50+ age group. In this case it shows us that people over 50 are 47% more likely to read paper X than the population as a whole. This is sometimes referred to as the index.

If you simply run your eye down the column for the over 50s, the percentages reflect what you saw in the total respondents table in terms of which paper has the largest number of readers but the percentages are now giving you more useful comparisons and you can use them to create new and useful measures. Paper Z has higher than average readers in the male and under-30 categories, while paper Y is stronger on women and 30–40-year-olds, and paper X is strongest on women and the over 50s.

Finally, if we look at percentages in a different direction we can add more to the picture.

Row percentages						
	All adults (%)	Male (%)	Female (%)	Age over 50 yrs (%)	Age 30 to 50 yrs (%)	Age 15 to 29 yrs (%)
Paper X	100	40	60	50	33	17
Paper Y	100	45	55	40	40	20
Paper Z	100	57	43	33	40	27
Total	100	49.5	50.5	34	41	25

Figure 6.8
Survey results –
version 3.

Using the row percentages we can see what proportion of each newspaper's readership is divided into the different groups. It provides us with a new comparative measure helping us understand how the readers are spread across the age groups and between the genders. Interestingly, the index we calculated using the column percentages still works out using the row comparisons. Fifty per cent of paper X readers are over 50 years of age compared with 34% of the population as a whole. Fifty as a percentage of 34 is 50 divided by 34 divided by 100 (50 divided by 0.34) which equals 147.

By exploring figures in this way you can quickly see that the simplest tools are often the best. Size may be important but comparison tells you more. Simple percentages can give you good insights into a table and you can even measure just how big a bias is by creating an index.

Finally, the three tools you may find most useful when looking at a table of figures are:

1   A pencil to circle really big or really small figures that might be worth taking note of.
2   A calculator to help you make simple calculations (percentages, for example).
3   A critical eye (what is this really telling me, what do *I* want to know from this?).

ACTION BOX 6.5

Using the report from Action Box 6.4, select some tables and use the rules above to extract additional useful information of use to you now but not present in the report's existing text.

Dumb statistics

Steer clear of averages, standard deviations, Chi-squared tests and all other statistical measures unless you are trained or know about such things. The worst statistics are those wrongly applied to useful data.

The most common culprit is the 'average'. Most people think they have some idea what an average is. They misuse the term and mislead themselves.

The most commonly used average is the arithmetic mean. It is a simple calculation where you add together a series of figures and divide the total by the number of figures in the series. Here is a simple example: 10 people's ages are 1, 3, 5, 5, 12, 35, 38, 40, 45 and 46. Add the ages together (total = 230) and divide by the number of people (10), 230 divided by 10 is 23. Accordingly, the average age of the group is 23. A simple statistic which is correct in every detail but both completely useless and misleading. The same average age could apply to a group of 10 people, five of whom were 22 and the other five were 24. Equally, they could all be aged 23, or four could be 56 years old and six aged 1 year.

In numeracy surveys the most common assumptions are that the average is the most common occurrence of something (this is the *mode*), that it is the midpoint in a set of figures (this is called the *median*) but few know how to calculate any of these forms of average. The simple guideline here is: if you do not have a clear and properly understood reason for using a statistical measure, *do not use it*.

COMMUNICATING FINDINGS

We have spent this chapter exploring some of the sources, tools and techniques you will need to collect in order to make sense of customer information. The rules and guidelines we have covered also apply to how you present your findings to others. Here is a summary of how to apply these guidelines to reporting and presenting what you have learned from your research.

- Keep it simple.
- Do not make assumptions you cannot support with evidence.
- Do not base important decisions on unreliable data.
- Do not present large detailed tables.
- Always try to keep focused.
- Say one thing at a time.
- Always give references/origins of data.
- Always show the size of samples used.
- Do not use more than one data set in the same table.
- Never add together data from different sources.

We will add to this and explore issues such as graphics in later chapters.

ACTION BOX 6.6

Revisit a report you have written in the last year and improve the tables and charts using the information in this chapter.

Conclusions

Research provides a wide range of opportunities for you to discover more about your customers. These opportunities do not need to be formally designed and expensive to use but the approach you adopt needs to be practical and rational. Furthermore, the data presented to and by managers can be simplified and made more accessible with very little statistical or mathematical expertise. Following a set of basic guidelines and avoiding complex or unreliable data or analyses will always ensure that the information you use is both reliable and informative.

Competence self-assessment

1 Select a TV advertisement for a product or service you use and identify what sort of research might have been used to help the advertisers target the advertisement, develop its message and measure its impact. Explain why you think this.
2 Describe three ways in which you think you could find out more about one of your suppliers.
3 How could research be used to improve the cost effectiveness of one area of your department's activities.
4 Identify a problem with an external customer that you think would be best solved with the use of research. What sort of research would you commission from a research agency and how would you judge their proposals?
5 Give five reasons why a statistic quoted on an advertisement and one quoted by a politician in the media cannot be wholly trusted. What do you need to know in order to trust it?

REFERENCES

Peters, T. and Austin, N. (1986) *A Passion for Excellence, The Leadership Difference*. Glasgow: William Collins.

Peters, T. (1987) *Thriving on Chaos: Handbook for a Management Revolution*. London: Pan.

CHAPTER 7

Marketing — conversing with customers

By exploring the tools available to respond to what we have learned, it is possible to identify internal and external processes that will take advantage of that knowledge to meet all of the aims and objectives. Here we examine the way we talk to customers and open up the dialogue that is the basis of new and long-lasting relationships with customers. Strangers cannot be loyal, relationships are not built with faceless organizations.

If we are to meet our customers' needs it is clearly not enough to concentrate on telling them things. We need to listen and respond. We need to get to know them and allow them the opportunity to get to know us; we need to have the most appropriate and advantageous relationship possible with our customers.

The sort of relationship will be determined by the sort of organization we are in, the sort of customers we are serving, the sort of relationship we currently have with them and what we (and they) want as a relationship in future. Generally, relationships seldom stay the same. Your definition (and that of your customers) of a 'good' relationship will change and the opportunities open to you will also change. You need to be clear of your objectives and use the tools available to you to help you bring about the best relationship possible at any given time.

In the next chapter we will explore issues such as performance and satisfaction measures in more detail. Here we will concentrate on communications and dialogue that help you communicate, exchange and build and strengthen relationships with your customers. Although there will be a few areas of overlap, we will split this chapter into conversing with *external* and *internal* customers.

EXTERNAL CUSTOMER COMMUNICATIONS

We will look at the way we communicate with our customers at three levels. This is simply a convenient way of explaining things and you will see that we are most likely to conduct a wide range of conversations at different levels with customers during any given period.

The three levels are *'from a distance'*, *'keeping in touch'* and *'talking together'*. We will explore the use of various media as we look at each level and show how, in a number of cases, the same medium might also work on different levels at the same time.

From a distance

The traditional approach to communications are well rooted within many organizations. We have explored a number of these in earlier chapters as the following summary shows:

Organizations communicate with external customers through:

- *Advertising* – General advertising and specific campaigns to support seasonal or other activities such as sales.
- *Sales contacts* – Either directly through their own sales force or via a retail system and may include leaflets, brochures and point-of-sales promotions. Non-commercial organizations usually have comparable routes for direct or indirect contact with customers. See other sections for more on this area.
- *Accounts* – Sales or other financial contact with customers.
- *After sales contact* – Warranties/guarantees, and similar services.
- *Complaints* – The point of contact for those with problems. This is explored in later sections.
- *Public relations* – Although a specialism, PR is another useful communications tool. The message is presented through reports, interviews and the use of news fed to selected media. Your message is part of the news received by current

and potential customers and can set your services or products in a useful context.

At this first level of contact with customers, organizations focus most of their communications' activity on advertising. Advertising is kept apart from the rest of the activities listed and direct contact is not the main objective. Although lines of communication from customers are available they are limited and passive in nature.

Advertising is aimed at target audiences and has the following functions to perform:

- *Compete* – To defend share of market, share of voice, and maintain position against competitors.
- *Find new customers* – To support the expansion of sales and replace lost or lapsed customers.
- *Inform* – To display wares, announce new products, services or features, keep characteristics and benefits in customers' minds.
- *Sales/retail support* – Bring customers to the door, show sales/retail that they have support, promote specific sales activities or launches.
- *Image* – Create and/or support product/brand image, perceptions, environment, aspirations, etc.
- *Generate interest/stimulate demand* – The general outcome of advertising, which can be capitalized on.

This approach helps organizations avoid developing a direct relationship with their customers. Customers develop relationships with the brand, product or service but have little engagement with the organization. In this way customers can be said to have a relationship with consumer products such as Heinz baked beans at the brand level. They like the taste but they also like the whole surrounding image and feel of the brand. It is even possible to have this relationship between a retail business and its customers. The customers see themselves as having strong links with the product/service/brand and may even feel strong ownership of it in some way but there is little actual dialogue between the two parties.

In this way, the advertising is constantly supporting and promoting the customer's experience while remaining separate from it. The customer's interaction is with the advertising and the product or service but not with the organization itself. Even the places where interaction between the customer and the organization are possible, little is made of them and continuation beyond that point is discouraged. In such circumstances it has been possible for organizations to have regular contact with customers and a long-term loyal customer base without the organization holding any notable records on these customers.

Of course, this approach was developed and persisted for two good reasons. First, it worked and in a number of cases it can still work today. Second, the technology was not developed or in place to consider other approaches. Once the first reason was shown to be untrue (or less accurate) and once people started to use new technology in this area, organization began to discover that even if the old ways still worked, they needed to do other things, too.

The media best suited to this purpose are broadcast media that reach a large number of people with each message. Television is the obvious choice with its limited ability to target small market segments, its large audiences and its ability to provide a colourful, life-filled message incorporating sound, movement, etc., in the message. National newspapers and magazines, commercial radio, cinema and posters are also candidate media for this approach. The advertising is characterized by limited or no feedback elements and requires no direct exchange or interaction with the target audience (except that they are encouraged to go out and buy, of course).

The communications programmes designed with these outcomes are either continuous or regular in nature. Once an organization has developed an image and begun to build on and use things such as brand characteristics it is difficult to even consider the risk of removing support for it or losing the position and image you have invested in for so long.

The balance in the programme is on the organization communicating to the customer or market. Customers are largely expected to be passive, communicating directly with the organization only for specific purposes such as when a problem arises or when financial or similar issues need to be resolved. Targeting is limited and more related to cost effectiveness in reaching customers rather than accuracy.

ACTION BOX 7.1

Identify a key aspect of your own communications that needs to be carried out from a distance. Describe what you need to communicate, who you need to communicate to, what media you wish to use and explain why.

Some notes on advertising

The standard communications models discussed in most marketing textbooks start with a one-way flow diagram showing how the message is carried to the customer using selected media and how, in the process, 'noise' (competing messages and conflicting information, etc.) can distort the message. When dealing with traditional concerns of mass marketing it was enough to explore how to maximize communication of the advertising message through the choice of media, targeting and message content. There are still a number of sectors where this approach continues to dominate the communications strategy of organizations and where the communication strategy has changed it is still a major component.

The 1980s and 1990s saw a major change in the media world. The world saw the fragmentation of broadcast media, with the effects of the introduction of new broadcast TV channels being dwarfed by the introduction of satellite and cable TV. In the UK a large number of new local radio stations were given airspace, and publishing technology made it possible to produce larger numbers of supplements and sections to newspapers as new, special interest magazines began to flood the market. This new technology also increased the range and types of poster sites available. A renewed interest in cinema was linked to new technology that allowed cinemas to have a larger number of smaller theatre spaces. This was linked to changes in shopping and lifestyle patterns that led to out-of-town shopping and large shopping malls where larger cinemas added to the opportunities to advertise.

The targeting of advertising using these media did not change quite as much as the media. Traditionally, advertising space in all media is based on research. A media owner needs to be able to prove to an advertiser that their medium reaches a verifiable number of people in the advertiser's target market. The cost effectiveness of advertising campaigns are, at least partly, calculated by working out the average cost per thousand people reached during the campaign. The aim is still to buy the maximum number of opportunities to reach the greatest proportion of your target market for the money you have available.

Targeting involved selecting the media most effective at reaching your target audience based on this research and then selecting appropriate editions, positions and times within the media where the target audience would most focus their attention, and where the editorial context was best suited to support the message you wished to put across. The advertising would reach a much wider audience than was actually intended but this was not seen as a major problem – even if your key customers made up more than 50% of your total customer base you still needed to communicate with your other customers, too.

Advertising used a mix of broadcast media with large audiences, together with some smaller, more specialist media. Today, the media broadcasting to larger audiences are still the most favoured but you need to use more to gain the same level of mass coverage as earlier, and you have more specialist media to choose from.

Although the objective of advertising is generally to help advertisers maximize sales of their products or services, advertising performs a number of other roles and has been judged on much wider criteria than sales for a long time. The simple cause and effect relationship between advertising and sales is often extremely difficult to understand or measure.

Advertising creates images, forms attitudes, develops expectations and supports the views and aspirations of both customers and the rest of the market-place. These other tasks for advertising mean that expensive cars are advertised to mass audiences to create and support the exclusive image of their products. The vast majority of the people who see the advertising will never be able to buy their products new but their aspirations and perceptions will support the reasons why the car manufacturer's customers will buy their products. In other words, they want everyone to know just how privileged and successful they are when they drive around in their new car. The advertising is there to support and boost the self-image of the purchasers in their neighbour's eyes as well as their own.

KEEPING IN TOUCH

Organizations of all sizes are communicating directly with their customers on an increasingly regular basis. This is partly because the technology and information systems that allow more direct and targetable communications have become more sophisticated and easier to use in the last two decades. It is also because communicating directly with customers has become more desirable and profitable as we have learned what to do and how to do it.

The hierarchy of communication approaches in this section is generally as follows:

Direct response advertising

The main points to consider with this basic form of direct marketing are:

- In this context we are mainly looking at the use of traditional media as outlined in the earlier section (TV, press, radio, etc.) but inserts in publications and a wide range of leaflets and point-of-sale materials also carry out much of this function effectively.
- This is often advertising with a more *traditional* purpose as outlined above but with a 'response mechanism' such as a coupon or phone number.
- It is frequently used as part of a *data gathering* programme collecting information on the market-place.
- It is also designed to *generate responses* as the first part of a series of communications growing from the potential customer's initial contact.

Targeted or direct communications

Another part of what is called direct marketing but where the communications are more narrowly targeted:

- *Direct mail* is targeted at existing or potential customers, again providing further opportunities to gather information but performing a powerful advertising role. It can employ a wide range of materials and technologies to add interest, entertain and create interest. It is usually carried out as part of a programme of communications with customer response as an essential element.
- *Telephone marketing* ranging from direct sales to surveys and customer-care follow-up calls. Again this is a form of direct communication with customers but with a different range of possible approaches and purposes. Sometimes leading to sales, often followed by other direct communications (direct mail or brochure) or with personal sales calls.

Established direct communications

- *Catalogue marketing* where a product range is published on paper and, increasingly, on the Web. The initial communications are generated by direct marketing activities and the process of communications develops as the customer uses the catalogue, buys goods, and receives offers, updates and new catalogues.
- *Direct mail programmes* These range from regular mailings based on seasonal or cyclical marketing activities (such as holidays, clubs, investment or insurance programmes, and so on) to the use of the medium as a promotional/advertising tool (alcohol and other product groups where advertising is restricted and existing users can be advertised to directly, pet products, baby products, etc. where knowledge of ownership or life-stage is known).

In all cases at this level the communications are characterized by accurate targeting, and encouraging and using customer response to build the programme of communications. It is still controlled and directed by the advertiser but individual customer knowledge is used and the processes driven by customer responses. Feedback is encouraged and used and communications continue directly with customers over time.

ACTION BOX 7.2

Identify a key aspect of your own communications that needs to be carried out adopting the approach outlined in the section above. Describe what you need to communicate, who you need to communicate to, what media you wish to use and explain why.

Talking together

The third level involves our customers in the process. This is both the newest and the oldest approach available. For organizations where it is possible to communicate directly with each of your customers and know them on a personal level it has always been the case that communications existed as a two-way process where either party could and would initiate the exchange. Mass markets turned this relationship into brand loyalty and new technology is beginning to make closer relationships possible as markets fragment and communications possibilities change.

Direct marketing has been causing part of this change as databases become larger, more detailed at a personal level and easier to manipulate and use cleverly. However, if all the communication initiatives are on the organization's side we can hardly claim that the communications are valid conversations or exchanges. Greater demands from customers and their increased sophistication are leading marketers in this area to use their data more subtly, build more narrowly targeted forms of communication and mix their media so that customers can begin to have a stronger and clearer voice. They are achieving this in a number of ways including developing specialist interest groups, clubs, product linking, and adding value through giving customers access across a wide range of media.

The Internet is where much of the new changes are taking place, while mobile communication and processing technologies are adding their possibilities to the process. In many ways the Internet is closer to a broadcast medium than it is to a direct medium. Information is available and accessible, organizations are open all the time, competition for attention is continuous and determined. It is possible to promote sites and features within sites on the internet, through e-mail and via all other media. Adding your website to all your communications including advertising on TV and posters has moved from an option to essential in just a few short years. Advertising without a web site address now looks odd.

However, sites are only accessed and navigated as a result of the customer's actions. Aggressive advertisers on the web are generally not well received (you can open a window on someone's screen but you cannot make them enter your site). Visits are customer initiated, being high on search engine results and being easy to find are as important as being easy to access and use. Integrating what you have in all of the different media accessible to customers is vitally important.

Customers are increasingly expecting to be able to interact with the message through interactive buttons on their remote controls, through texting and palm-held computers, personal organizers, laptops and personal computers. Additional information is the norm and instant access, maximum choice and fast delivery are expected outcomes.

What marketers described at the end of the twentieth century as relationship marketing is being transformed not simply by being able to build better and more sophisticated marketing databases and systems but by being able to use them and new technologies to allow greater levels of interaction between organizations and customers. The issue stops being one of trying to develop programmes that build specific types of relationship and becomes one of striving to understand what sort of relationship you can have with customers and how to nurture the most valuable ones.

ACTION BOX 7.3

Identify a key aspect of your own communications that needs to be carried out adopting the approach outlined in the section above. Describe what you need to communicate, who you need to communicate to, what media you wish to use and explain why.

COMPLAINTS – A WONDERFUL OPPORTUNITY TO REALLY COMMUNICATE

One area that persists as a key aspect of communications at this level and is either paid lip-service or stepped around by marketers is that of customer complaints. Every time a customer complains about a failure in your service or product you have the opportunity to either regain their custom while winning new customers or to lose both their custom and the custom of many of their friends and acquaintances. Later, we go into more detail on this subject but the ten rules are important here.

1 *Listen* to the complaint carefully.
2 Make sure you *understand* the problem and *check* with the complainant.
3 *Apologize* – and mean what you say! Try to deal with the customer as honestly and caringly as possible regardless of how upset or angry they are. Do not forget to *thank them* for telling you – if no one complains, the problems cannot be resolved.
4 *Explain* the process you are about to follow and tell them clearly what you are going to do next.
5 *Give them details*. Your details, details of relevant contacts, and information such as timings, etc.

6 *Do not promise what cannot be delivered!*

7 *Keep to your side of the agreement*, do what you have said you will do.

8 *Keep a clear record* of the complaint and what you have done to resolve the problem.

9 *Contact* the customer to keep them informed of progress and do it when you said you would.

10 *Make sure that it gets resolved.*

Why is complaints-handling such an important part of communicating with customers? Here are the details, the argument is clear and overwhelming:

■ In the UK only 4–5% of dissatisfied customers actually complain!

■ More importantly, for every one complaint around 26 probably want to and six are likely to have a serious complaint; one that you really need to know about.

■ Dissatisfied customers are likely to tell around 14 others about the problem.

■ Dissatisfied customers are not only unlikely to remain your customers, they will discourage other current customers from remaining loyal to you.

■ The cost of resolving a complaint is likely to be between 10 and 25% of the cost of finding a new customer.

■ Customers who complain and have their problems solved to their satisfaction invariably become very loyal customers.

■ These customers tend to recommend the organization to up to ten other potentially new customers.

The following section in this chapter explores communications with internal customers. Again, the lines between one area and another are for convenience and you will discover that much of what is said in both sections applies to both internal and external customers. Apply the principles and the results will follow.

General rules to apply to your communications

Before looking at internal communications in detail, certain guidelines should apply in all areas of communications with customers.

Advertising generally, and communications transmitted via a public carrier (postal systems, telecommunications, e-mail, and so on) require that the content of your message is *legal* (i.e. does not contravene local or national laws), *decent* (does not transmit or promote pornographic, violent or other abusive or inappropriate materials) and *honest* (it is not deliberately untruthful, deceitful, misleading, etc.).

Assuming that you always endeavour to meet these requirements, here are some notes designed to help you improve your communications.

You need to ask yourself whether your communication is:

Consistent?	*In message content* – Does not contradict what was said in other communications, etc.
	In style – Uses departmental and organization's house style, etc.
	In image – Presenting an image of you consistent with other communications.
Clear?	*Using simple language* – Keep your language simple, short sentences, jargon free, etc.
	One idea at a time – Do not mix up messages or ideas, avoid confusion and complexity wherever possible.
	Keep to your objectives – Have objectives for your communication and meet them.
	Have achievable outcomes – Objectives have to be achievable, on time, measurable, etc., and so do communications. Do not ask the impossible, be clear what is required by the communication.
Appropriate?	*To you* – Is the language, tone and style appropriate to who you are, your position and what you need to say?
	To the recipient – Is the language appropriate for the person or people you are talking to? How should they be addressed and how does this fit with you and the message?
	To the purpose – How formal/informal is the communication, what is its job, why are you sending it, and so on?
	For the medium – The language, style, etc. need to fit in with the medium you use. What is acceptable in a memo or e-mail will not be right for a letter, language for a contract is different to that used in an invitation, etc.

In its details – What additional information do you need to provide? Date, return details, your title, reference numbers, etc?

Timely? *For action* – Can the recipient do what is required on time? Does your communication give them adequate notice? If it is to secure a meeting or appointment is the lead time long enough?

For response – If you need an answer have you given enough time for this to be done?

Other important considerations affecting how you communicate include:

Media requirements – The details about yourself, your department, and so on, will vary according to the medium you use. In addition to those provided as standard you may wish to add other details for particular recipients. For example, your direct line or mobile number, room number and so on. Reference details and other useful details might also be appropriate. You should always add the return address to the outside of envelopes when using postal services but this may not be needed for internal post, nor will it be needed in most e-mail systems.

Confidentiality clauses and other similar additions to communications are sensibly added when using e-mails but might be added to other communications, too.

Always make certain that the recipient knows *who has sent the message*! Sign all your communications, tell people who you are when you contact them by telephone, introduce yourself in meetings and presentations and do the same in other situations where people are new to you or are uncertain of your name or position.

Always keep a *record of communications* and keep your records organized in a way that ensures you can refer to them easily at a later date. Records include storing copies in appropriate folders, files, etc., keeping responses together with your original communications and ensuring that those who need to know about these communications know where to find them and can have proper access to them when required. Records of your telephone and face-to-face communications are best kept in a personal notebook – more official records can then be made from your personal notes.

> ### ACTION BOX 7.4
>
> Select one internal and one external communication you have been responsible for or know well. Analyse them using the guidelines above and identify any issues or difficulties that would have been avoided if these had been applied at the time of the communications' design. How might you improve them now?

INTERNAL CUSTOMER COMMUNICATIONS

Now that we have dealt with basic communications let us look at internal communications in more detail.

Communications in this area of customer relations are carried out across three broad levels whose borders are less well defined. As with other communications, this is a convenient way of dividing them and much communication takes place on several levels at the same time. Our three divisions or levels are '*Talking to*', '*Exchange*' and '*Feedback*'.

Talking to your customers may invite feedback and most likely will include details for this purpose, but the primary purpose of the communication will be to pass on information, instructions or complete an exchange (i.e. formal agreement, confirm conclusions, provide minutes or contact reports, send reports, etc.). Here are some brief notes on the media most commonly used at this level:

- *Message boards* – These perform a number of useful functions. They are public spaces where news, information and announcements can be made, and where other members of staff and some customers can participate. Can also be part of the exchange and feedback loops. Can be in a physical location in or near your office or on the intra or internet.
- *Newsletters* – Performing the same sort of functions as message boards but more formal in content and production. Can be used to involve customers and staff while controlling the flow of information, its themes, style and content. More easily used to promote the department or organization to external as well as internal customers, more intimate and easily controlled than public relations efforts through independent media. Can be as detailed and professional or as simple and 'home-made' as you require. Can involve staff and customers in production as well as content while remaining under your direct control.

■ *E-mail/letters/memos* – Included here as direct media where you can choose the level and/or type of feedback you wish to invite. Can be used to announce or provide information, etc. Can also be the vehicle for delivering other messages (reports, newsletters, etc.) and can invite feedback to or herald communication from another person or location (letters on behalf of sales or other staff, introducing a new service, etc.).

■ *Formal meetings and presentations* – There may be face-to-face meetings where it is not really appropriate for those attending to provide feedback there and then.

The level where you do not expect or require response helps to define the style and content of the communications.

Exchange with your customers is the level where dialogue with your customers is built into the communication process – this can be either formal or informal in nature. The importance is in providing the means for that exchange within the communication itself. Here are examples:

■ *Formal e-mail/telephone/letters/memos* – Where the purpose is to elicit a response or exchange and where the customer's part is determined by the content of the communication. This is most often the case with e-mail, letters and memos but there are many telephone conversations in this category, too. Sales and research or information-gathering calls are often structured and planned in this way and many are recognized as such by customers who find it easiest and most convenient to comply with the purpose of the communication by giving the information required or purely acting on the order, etc.

■ *Informal e-mail/telephone/letters/memos* – What distinguishes these from more formal communications is the looser structure. Although lacking formal constraints may suggest these to be less important, they are actually extremely important. They cannot take place without first establishing a good relationship with the customer and they have their own set of rules defined by the level and type of relationship you have. They provide information not accessible any other way and establish trust and links that are invaluable in all management roles.

■ *Formal meetings and presentations* – Many formal meetings are built around the structured exchange between two or more parties rather than to inform the other party. Of course, you can plan question and answer sessions into presentations and have formal feedback sessions or distribute questionnaires to obtain feedback.

- *Informal meetings* – There are a variety of types of informal meeting where the communications notes for other informal communications apply. They may include lunches/dinners/parties/receptions or other get-togethers. They further relationships while ensuring exchange of ideas, views, agreements and alliances.

Feedback is the level or type of communication you design for the customer to talk to you. You may include some message you wish to promote as part of the whole package (text on a leaflet or questionnaire, for example) and the context of the feedback will always tell your customer something about you (how you care, etc.) but it is their route to telling you things. Here are some examples:

- *Questionnaires and other feedback forms* – These are not just for external customers. After presentations given to groups of your internal customers you should distribute feedback forms (how good were you, did you cover everything, what else should you cover, what next?). Services you provide can be improved with the help of customer feedback and so on.
- *Suggestion boxes* – Not just for the factory floor, these can provide customers (and staff) with the opportunity to make constructive suggestions and criticism. The biggest problem managers have with them is not the negative or unpleasant material they expect to receive but the fact that they receive very little through them. Once established and when connected with award schemes they can work extremely well.
- *Surveys* – Covered in an earlier chapter this is a structured and carefully planned approach to feedback which applies to internal as much as external customers.
- *Reviews* – These are a useful way of providing customers with a formal and powerful way of telling you what they think. They supplement the feedback you have all year round but you can structure them to cover all of the areas of concern for both parties, which can lead to renewed commitments, contracts and an improved basis for cooperation for the next period.
- *Quality circles and teams* – Where you bring together staff and customers to help review and rethink different aspects of

what and how you serve customers. As part of your quality plan, these groups work together on chosen issues and report back to you and the rest of the team with ideas, suggestions and new approaches.

■ *Brainstorming* – One of a number of techniques you can employ to help you involve your customers in reviewing and rethinking what you provide to them. The meeting is informal in nature but the structure allows the members to push the boundaries of their thinking about your products or services. As customers, their perspective will open up new possibilities which you might never think of and will be critically evaluated by those you would provide the new services to.

ACTION BOX 7.5

Identify three different internal communications – one that fits each of the three categories above – and use the notes in the section to see how you might improve or add value to these communications. What can you use in other communications you are currently planning?

CHOOSING YOUR RELATIONSHIPS

We have been looking at how we communicate with our customers and allow them to communicate with us. Linked with the idea of communicating with customers is the idea that we have some sort of relationship with them. Earlier sections have touched on this and illustrated how different types of communication help to develop different types of relationship. To meet your customers' needs you need to be able to understand the sort of relationship you have with your customers. Here are some of the types of relationship you might have with your customer. Much of what you have looked at so far will tell you the sorts of relationships you have with your customers. Do not be surprised if they are not included here, following chapters explore this further. These are relationships as seen from the provider's point of view:

■ *Frequency* – The relationship as defined by how frequently the customer uses the service or buys the product. What is defined by frequent will vary between organizations (a car manufacturer's frequent customer might buy once every 1–3 years, while a supermarket customer might buy daily or weekly). The organization sets the levels to define types of relationships. Is your service being habitually used, is it being actively sought on a regular basis? Frequency is the first pointer but you will need more information to understand it further. Frequent travellers are actively sought and rewarded by airlines but what else do they look for in a customer?

- *Value* – Again defined by the organization. It can be a mistake to judge the importance of customers based purely on the value of their purchases. Allocating resources and efforts to those already spending a large amount may seem a good strategy but reliance on a small number of large-value customers can also be risky (losing one customer can be disastrous). Better to develop relationships that encourage increased use across customers at all value levels. *Value* can also refer to the value of the product or service. The relationships defined by the value of what is being bought range from the exclusive, high value to the low-value, mass market relationship.

- *Satisfaction* – Many organizations will measure the level of satisfaction expressed by their customers and use this to guide improvements in their products and services. Some also use the measure to help them identify groups with different types of relationships with the organization. Communications, reward systems and offers are then based on which group the customer is in.

- *Attitude/image* – Customers' attitudes towards the organization or what it provides can help determine the relationships they will have with the organization. This has already been explored in the context of brands but it is also evident in the way people approach and buy from certain organizations. Customers may be willing to pay a premium for products or services from certain companies based on the attitudes they have or image they have of the organization.

- *Aspiration* – Often linked to attitude and image, the aspirations of customers may determine both the suppliers they choose and the type of products or services they buy. Organizations take advantage of this in a number of ways. For example, completely new products are often priced at a premium price because they are new and can command a high price from those customers who constantly seek to have the newest things first. Small production levels of high-value items help recoup some of the cost of development while preparing the product for increased production levels. The relationship between producers and the different groups of customers in this context is based on their aspirations.

■ *Needs* – This area was explored in Chapter 2. Relationships with customers can be based purely on their level of need. This can be at the material or physical level (utilities companies serve their customers' basic needs and the starting point for the relationship is likely to be this need), the emotional level (the art and entertainments sectors are good examples as they develop relationships with customers whose needs are deeply emotional) but it also includes intellectual, spiritual, political and aspirational needs.

■ *Fit* – This basis for a relationship could be interpreted in the context of clothing or other physical attributes but it more usually refers to other attributes of the customer. These include demographic, economic, geographical and sociological fits with those of the product or service. For example, baby products are unlikely to be of interest or use to people completely unconnected with babies, and mountain-climbing gear will have a similarly self-defining market. The relationships built between organizations and customers on the basis of fit are determined by the appropriateness of the product or service to the situation of the customers. It can be deeply linked with need but is also linked with a number of the other attributes defining relationships. So, aspiration and need as defined by fit will determine the potential for the relationship.

■ *Market size* – This may be linked with other aspects such as value, fit or aspiration. The size of the market may determine the level of personal involvement between customer and supplier. Consider the differences: the relationship between an architect who designs a block of flats and the flat dwellers is different to that of the architect who is commissioned to build a person's house; the differences in relationships between a customer buying meat from a local butcher and a customer buying meat from a supermarket. Size matters.

■ *Commitment (loyalty)* – Usually a combination of a number of the other characteristics identified here. Rewarding loyalty often means rewarding use in terms of frequency and/or value but this is also divided into product or service preference and some indicators regarding the customer's personal circumstances (known income, marital status, number of children, social class, etc.).

The communications' strategies help shape and nurture the relationships by first setting the scene, building the image and awareness, attracting groups of similar people, handling their pre- and post-purchase actions and feelings, supporting and enhancing feelings, dealing with problems if they arise, reassuring customers, keeping them in touch and informed, giving them reasons to continue in addition to the product or service, rewarding and developing other ways of recognizing, listening and responding, finding more like them, attracting back lapsed or lost customers. The type of product or service, type of market and relationships all contribute to the way in which we apply this pattern of communication, which parts we leave out, which new ideas we add in.

ACTION BOX 7.6

Choose one internal and one external customer group and identify the different types of relationships you have with them. List how these are supported or served by the communications you use.

Competence self-assessment

1 Select a product/service you know well or use and describe what you believe to be the main characteristics of its key customers. Using advertisements for this product/service say which characteristics/customer groups are being targeted and why you think this.
2 Using your bank for this exercise, how many different forms of communication can you say you have received from this organization in the last month? Include general advertising as well as direct communications. How effective has each been and why?
3 Identify one good and one bad communication you have received at home and use the general rules of communication to explain why they were good or bad.

4 Using a department you work closely with, identify three important ways they communicate with you. What other three ways not currently used by them would improve communications further?
5 Identify a good and a bad experience you have had with a key customer group. How do these reflect the type of relationship you have with the customer groups and what other relationships could you develop that would improve things?

CHAPTER 8

Marketing — measuring all that is important

Measuring and evaluating are not add-ins, they are part of the process. Simple, effective and relevant measures add to efficiency, identify problems early, avoid major problems, improve internal as well as external customers' experiences. Success without measures is difficult to repeat, hard to improve on, impossible to share effectively. Quality applies to the whole process and those involved as well as in the resulting product or service.

WHY MEASURE?

Even if you feel you already know the answer it is worth reviewing why we measure aspects of what we do and how people experience our products and services.

There are five reasons why we measure and we will use these to help us focus on the virtuous cycle of measurement. This cycle will help you maximize the way you meet your customer needs.

The five reasons are:

1 *Maintain and improve quality* – The quality of your products or services cannot be taken for granted. You need to monitor quality, review it, work with others to improve it and always strive to improve it. It is never good enough simply

to be better than current competitors or better than you were last year.

2 *Increase efficiency and improve performance* – Efficiency depends on measurement. How well are you doing things, where can you make improvements, what additional things can you do now that you are working more efficiently?

3 *Maximize value for both you and your customers* – Value can be a comparative measure; for example, what do you get out compared to what you put in? This measure is important to your customer but it is also important to you, your staff, organization and suppliers.

4 *Increase and secure customer satisfaction* – Knowing what value customers get from what you provide does not tell you how they feel about it. Satisfaction, as we have already noted, is based on expectations as well as experience.

5 *Develop and maintain customer commitment* – Success is based on securing tomorrow's customer today. Will our customers come back to us? How many will there be? What is their level of commitment to us? Knowing something about this tells us what to do next and tells us how well 1 to 4 above are working for us.

These apply to the internal as well as the external market and, although competition may not have the same sort of influence or effect on the internal market, the reasons and outcomes remain vitally important.

MEASURING WITHIN A CYCLE OF IMPROVEMENT

The reasons in our introduction form what we call a virtuous cycle. Figure 8.1 illustrates this cycle and shows how communications and support services link within the cycle to help it work, while competition from outside remains an important external influence on the cycle.

The cycle was developed from examining the relationship between quality and customer satisfaction. Although it is clear that a relationship between the two exists, it is possible to have both a high level of satisfaction within your customer base and products or services that enjoy a high level of quality, but still suffer from high turnover of customers indicating low commitment. It became clear that value

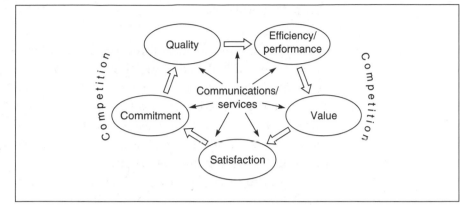

Figure 8.1
The cycle of
quality /
satisfaction
improvement.

was also part of the equation and that value worked both ways. In order for customers to experience products or services positively they needed to have clear and positive experiences of value. In order to ensure the experience, those providing the added value needed to feel that it was positive for them as well – companies needed to believe that it was worth investing in and staff needed to enjoy satisfaction and benefits from their extra efforts, etc. On one side of the equation it became obvious that value had to grow out of more than just improved quality; you needed improvements in efficiency and performance to enable the improvements to take place and deliver them effectively. On the other side, the cumulative effect of these improvements helped to secure commitment. In some cases, the improvements in efficiency led to opportunities to support the process of customer commitment through better after-sales services, etc.

So, what we discover is a cyclical process of improvement where the positive outcomes are found within the organization as well as in customer attitudes and behaviour. Additional improvements are usually increased competitiveness, improved efficiency and higher returns. There are no secret ingredients in the process but it does require that managers have some measure of what is happening throughout the cycle.

The question is not 'why measure?' but 'what things should we measure and how?'

ACTION BOX 8.1

Select one product or service you are responsible for and identify how a virtuous cycle of improvement might apply to it.

What to measure

In earlier chapters we examined the route from source to customers and the part you played along that route. We have divided our focus for measurement into three areas and you will see how these fit within that model. We will look at each area in turn and refer to the general model of the route. From this you will be able to identify where you need to focus in order to develop your own programme of measuring and monitoring for improvement.

The guiding principles we will apply here are:

- What will I/my department be judged on?
- What do we control, what can we change or influence?
- What can we measure that will tell us how well we are currently performing?
- What can we measure that will help us understand what we need to improve?

Some of your key measures will encompass all of these principles at the same time. If you focus on just one area and fail to choose measures that encompass all four principles you risk under-performing or failing in your role.

After reviewing all of the possible measures available to you, it will become clear that several measures are all doing the same or a very similar task. You will need to select the best for any given job. If one area requires four different measures and another area requires only one, that will reflect the current situation in each area. Prudent reviews of measures will lead you to change and refine the process from time to time.

Products/services

This includes the following areas. Some, perhaps many, will not apply to your situation and there may be other categories you can add that would fit into this area:

- Raw materials.
- Part and fully finished products.
- Wrapping/packaging materials.
- Presentation materials.

- Internal information.
- Services/products for internal customers.
- Services/products for/from external partners.
- Services/products for external customers.

Measures in this area could include any of the following:

- *Physical inspection* – Everything you are involved in producing or providing deserves regular inspection. Services involve a range of materials (written, on-line, printed, and so on) in order for the service to be provided, promoted, etc. There are people who present the services and people who are involved in the supply indirectly. What can you judge from what you see and how can you measure it in order to monitor changes and improvements? These are mainly what we describe as *quality* measures.
- *Testing* – After looking, how well does it work? You may have reports on this but have you tried it for yourself? Is your information good enough and can you interpret it better if you know what the measure is like as a customer, enquirer, user? These can be *quality* measures but may include *satisfaction* or *value* indicators. Testing may also indicate an important *efficiency* measure.
- *Timing* – This may provide *efficiency* and *value* measures for internal concern while indicating possible measures of *satisfaction* and *value* for customers.
- *Measuring costs* – Depending on where the costs are, you could be measuring anything from the customer's view of *value* to *quality* or *efficiency* measures.
- *Measuring resources* – What does it take to produce/provide the service or product? How has this changed and why? This may start as an *efficiency* measure and provide a way of measuring *value*.
- *Internal views* – For those products or services being provided to external customers, what can we discover about how internal players view what we are currently providing? Are they satisfied with it, what do they want to improve? Internal *satisfaction* reviews can provide valuable insights and measures.
- *Customer views* – They can tell you what they think of *quality*, *value*, their level of *satisfaction* and *commitment* to the product or service.

■ *Comparative measures* – How does the product/service in question compare with similar or alternative sources/supplies, competitors? Any of the above areas can be used for comparison.

Your analyses of your customers and their needs will provide you with the objectives, strategy and plan, and your selection of measures will help you guide, monitor and evaluate the actions you take.

ACTION BOX 8.2

Review your product/service using the list above and identify what measures you already have in place, what you should consider adding and explain what they will help you achieve.

Processes

Behind the services and products above are the processes that deliver them. These include:

- Buying.
- Production processes.
- Packing.
- Transport/distribution.
- Warehousing/storage.
- Delivery.
- Communications.
- Information provision.
- Third-party activities.
- Customer care.
- Complaint/problem processing.

Common or popular points where measures are taken in this area include:

■ *Links in the chain* – You have already counted the links so what else can you look at? You can measure the time taken at each link, the cost and resources used and the value added at each stage. *Efficiency* and *value* are the two main aspects listed here.

- *Delays* – The number, the length and the location of delays affect what we measure in terms of *efficiency* and *satisfaction* but their nature and the stage where the delays occur can also affect *quality* and *value*.
- *Problems* – Categorize, classify, measure the cost, importance, impact of problems and where they occur. Allocate to the relevant stage in the cycle.
- *Goodwill hunting* – Can you identify stages in any of the relevant processes where people carry out actions that are not specified or official but add useful or significant value to what the customer ultimately receives? People add value through goodwill or necessity and the actions are added in with the original processes. Often these additions are not noticed until a detailed review takes place or staff changes occur. *Quality* and *efficiency* can be measured by the number and type of informal additions and changes that have taken place since the last time someone reviewed the system.
- *Age and number of stages* – When were each of the stages in the process reviewed and when were they updated? A process may not need changing but if it is never reviewed how will you know? Changes to one stage can cause changes to be needed in other stages.
- *Date last reviewed* – See above.
- *Equipment or resources* – Evaluation of quality, age, efficiency and performance of these should be carried out. This is common in industrial contexts but less well catered for in office and other service situations. Computer or telecommunications failure should be predictable and avoidable. Furniture, lighting and other environmental resources need to be monitored and can affect the *efficiency* and *well-being of staff* providing important services.
- *Stability* – One of the aspects of reliability which affect *efficiency* and *quality* and will ultimately affect *satisfaction*. Stability can be measured by the amount of pressure or problems required to cause a link in the customer chain to fail.
- *Support/back up* – Where and how much back-up can you find in the system? Too much and you have an inefficient system, too little and it is prone to failures.
- *Effectiveness* – The amount of output compared to the amount of effort taken. There are a number of ways this is measured (man hours per unit of output or units of output per man hour, for example).

As with products and services, the aspects measured are determined by the processes you manage or rely on and the nature of your activities and customers.

ACTION BOX 8.3

Identify the key measures you currently use in this area and select three new ones that would add significantly to your performance.

Players

Most of us will be able to identify players in all of the categories below but do not worry if some are not relevant or simply not important to you and your activities. The list, like the others, is a starting point and guide. Most managers can identify the following players:

- External supplier.
- Internal suppliers.
- You/your department.
- Internal customers.
- External partners.
- External customers.
- Competitors/alternative sources.

When considering what to measure and how to measure it you may look at much of the following:

- *Last reviewed/asked* – You should have a definable relationship with all of the players you think are important to you. Internal as well as external players need to be part of your communications, research and review programmes. How frequently do you schedule these in and when was the last time? Can you relate to this the quality of service you give or receive? Levels of communication can relate to all aspects from *quality to commitment* and need to be tracked if not measured.
- *Training* – The level of training of players (this can include customers) can be an indicator on a number of levels.
- *Experience* – Like training, experience can be an important indicator or predictor on a number of levels.

- *Satisfaction* – It is important to try to measure and monitor satisfaction levels within the other groups of players as well as within customer groups. For example, *satisfaction* within your department may determine levels of *efficiency* and satisfaction within supplier groups may indicate expected levels of *quality*.

- *Output versus input* – What do people put into their work and what do you get out? This may be 'hard measures' such as time and numbers of units or 'soft measures' such as how much effort they feel they are putting in and how satisfied customers feel. Although this can measure aspects of any of the levels, it is most used in measures of *value* and *commitment*.

- *Commitment* – Alongside combined measures above, you can ask people just how committed they feel and what they feel committed to.

- *Cost* – Where do the major costs within your product or service lie and what does that tell you? What can you vary or influence and how would that affect the outcome? Looking at the figures will help answer that question. Look at less obvious costs such as staff turnover and what that means in terms of both satisfaction and additional costs. Measuring can validate new approaches to old problems.

- *Image* – Your department's image as seen by you and your staff versus other players. For example, how much do you need to know to understand or influence commitment and motivation from staff, suppliers and customers?

- *Feelings, attitudes and preferences* – As with *image*, you should invest time in finding out the feelings, attitudes and preferences of all the player groups and monitor how changes in these affect other aspects of your work with them.

- *Value* – Direct questions on the subject of value should also be considered within each group.

- *Length of commitment/involvement* – Direct questions about commitment are useful, but simple measures such as how long they have been customers or suppliers need to be looked at, too. Low feelings of commitment from a new customer may be seen as an opportunity but low levels in long-standing customers should be seen as a problem.

- *Comparisons* – Some comparisons are immediately obvious (such as the previous example). However, if you are gathering and monitoring information from a number of sources you need to invest some time to look at how the data compare. Two sources of similar data should produce similar results, for example, and differences can often provide important additional information. Similarly, you would be unwise to insist on ignoring a number of different sources all telling you the same story.

ACTION BOX 8.4

Put together a table with your key players as columns, and areas to measure as rows, then identify which areas are measured, how they are measured and what needs to be added to improve your management in this area.

MAKING SENSE OF YOUR OPTIONS

The first part of this chapter has focused on the range and types of options open to managers wishing to use measures to improve their effectiveness in meeting customer needs.

In order to select the best measures for your particular situation use the work you have completed on your route to customers to help you prioritize what you need to know and why. Taking each of the stages from *quality* to *commitment* in the cycle in Figure 8.1, review what information you currently use, collect or have access to. Separate these into the headings 'Products/services', 'Processes' and 'People', and see what you currently know under each heading. Use Figure 8.2 as a template to help you write down this information and list the measures you currently have in each of these areas. How useful are

Quality		Measures	
	Current known position	Currently have/use	Missing/need
Products/ services			
Processes			
People			

Figure 8.2 Assessment tables.

they? Do they tell you what you need to know? What is missing that would definitely help you in this area? What do you need to find out and from whom?

By working through each of the stages of the cycle you will begin to find a pattern with key players, processes and stages repeating themselves and key pieces of information appearing as important. Your objective is not to amass a huge number of measures across all areas but to find the most useful, most important measures for you and your department.

Once you have listed the known and missing elements, use your objectives from Chapter 5 to select the ones you want to prioritize, mark them out using a highlighter pen, or highlight them on the screen. Use your objectives to help you refine your selected measures. If you find that you have missed something out or have not covered a relevant key objective, add it in now.

You now have a clearer idea of what you need to measure and why. In Chapter 6 we looked at how to refine the questions you want to ask. The following section builds on this to help you measure and monitor effectively.

How to measure

We will review four aspects of measuring in this section: how to collect your own information using *questionnaires* and *forms*, how to find and make sense of what is already available to you by using *existing data sources*, how to make use of your and your staff's daily interactions with customers and suppliers (*informal sources*); and using simple tools (such as *tables*, *charts*, etc.) to make sense and best use of your information.

Questionnaires and forms

Asking customers and suppliers questions can be surprisingly easy and as long as you keep it simple it should be quite painless. Here are some guidelines.

The approach

- *Who?* – Think carefully about who you want to complete your questionnaire or form. It may be attractive to ask all of your customers but if there are thousands and your budget is limited you will have to revise your thinking. Unless you are planning to use a research agency it is best to keep what you do as simple as possible. If you can handle printing, distributing and collecting a few hundred responses and you believe it to be important, decide how many you can do and distribute them evenly across your customer base. Resources and practicalities will determine how you decide this. If you are considering a relatively small group but do not want to approach them all, think carefully how you can divide the group into sub-groups and ask a few within each sub-group (split by high, medium and low value, or by region, for example). You may want to ask only those who buy regularly or who use particular products or services, and you can use their own actions to select them by including the questionnaire with the product or at the point of delivery of the service.

■ *When?* – Timing may be important. You may only want them to respond at the point when a service or product is delivered or used, or you may want to question them only when they are in a particular place or at a particular point in their usage of your product or service. Timing might also be important for certain groups you are interested in – seasonal use or use at different times of the day or week, for example.

■ *How?* – Traditionally, you would send forms or questionnaires along with letters, or have forms or leaflets included with other literature or in the packaging (perhaps associated with the warranty or guarantee), distributed at point of sale or in a special location (the reception or guest room in a hotel, for example). Using new technology you can fax, e-mail, place on your web site or even text customers/suppliers with suitable questions or forms, include them as part of the contents of a CD, DVD, disk or within interactive TV programmes.

■ *Formats* – Regardless of the medium you use to place questions in front of customers, there are some basic things you need to do. The questions need to be introduced properly by inviting the person to take part, by explaining why you are asking the questions and what the outcome of the exercise will be. You may even have an incentive you can offer to encourage response (favourites are money-off coupons, free or reduced-price products or service from your organization and a prize draw for something substantial). The questionnaire should be easy to complete, well tested and free of difficult to understand or difficult to answer questions and it should not take very long to complete (it is a good policy to tell them how long it will take – if you are embarrassed to tell them, the questionnaire is probably too long!). Do not forget to *thank* them at the end of the form or questionnaire. If you can, tell them you will send them a summary of the results, too.

- *Response management* – Responses need to be collected or sent to you before you can use them. Remember this when planning the exercise. Provide stamped addressed envelopes or some other means to ensure response. Fax-back is a good approach and so is the use of e-mail with a 'response return' element. If forms are being distributed at specific locations you can provide a suitable box or provide staff in those locations with the means to gather and return the completed forms to you.

Be aware that you will need to be able to analyse the information you gather so consider how you are going to do this while you are designing the questionnaire. Responses from simple questionnaires can be entered on to a spreadsheet and analysed easily. More complex ones may be better handled using a database package. There are a number of companies who produce easy-to-use software that allows you to create a questionnaire, enter the responses and analyse it using one package.

The questions

There are basic things you should always remember about questions. Once you have decided what you want to ask and refined the questions to make them as clear and unambiguous as possible, you still need to check them for the following. Are your questions:

- *Short and meaningful?* – Keep the questions short and sharp, use simple language and keep the response options to the minimum possible making sure that your questions and invited responses are not leading (do not put words into your respondents' mouths), that you have covered all the options (no matter how positive your responses are, if you failed to offer them the chance to give you negative responses the results will not be believed) and that all of the questions are relevant to the respondents as well as to you.

■ *Closed?* – Open-ended questions are harder to analyse, more ambiguous, often fail to get all the information required, take longer to complete and are frequently poorly responded to. Closed questions, where respondents only have to tick or cross off boxes to answer questions are easier for people to complete and much easier to analyse. Unless you have a very good reason to do otherwise, stick to closed questions and test them on staff, colleagues, family and friendly customers/ suppliers before committing to them.

■ *Using easy to use scales?* – If you want relative measures (How much do you agree with this? How much did you like this? – and so on) keep your scale to five points with 'very, quite, neither, not quite and not very' as the model of your positive to negative range. If you want people to rank attributes keep the list short and if you have a long list get them to select the top three or five from that list if you can. Never make things more complicated, always try to find the simplest solution as that will be the easiest to answer, the simplest to analyse and will end up being the most meaningful to you.

■ *The right size?* – Only you will know what the right size is but if the questions take longer than a few minutes to answer it is probably too long. If you need a really long and detailed questionnaire it might be better for you to employ a research company to carry out a professional survey. Even if you think you can get away with it, think carefully before subjecting prized customers or suppliers to a long and complicated questionnaire.

The analysis

Measuring in this context should require very basic forms of analysis. You are seeking measures such as 'how satisfied are my customers with X or Y service?' or 'do my suppliers prefer order form A or B?' or possibly 'how does my product compare with the equivalent competitor products?' Levels of response to succinct questions and simple percentages are what you require.

Once you have established your base set of data you can repeat the exercise at relevant intervals (monthly, quarterly, etc.) in order to monitor changes but the first analysis will set the pattern for the whole process so keep the analysis as simple as you kept the questions.

Some people even use the format of the questionnaire to record the responses (i.e. percentages slotted into each response box within the questionnaire) while others record them as a set of tables. Let your use of the results define how you approach the analysis.

Finally, you may consider it worth while to write up the results as a short report for your superiors or colleagues. Think carefully about this before committing yourself and decide at that point whether you want to have the report as a one-off or something you will repeat.

ACTION BOX 8.5

Select one of your key customer groups and work out how you could apply the exercise above. Test the approach to see how you could use the improvements in other areas.

Existing data sources

Not all of the measures you need will be available from survey data. Here are some other sources you should consider; and spend a short time looking at the sources outlined in Chapters 2 and 6.

- *Records* – You will have access to a wide range of records including files on sales, purchases, time and resources spent on various activities, numbers and types of people employed in relevant activities, numbers of enquiries, complaints and so on. Use these sources to answer some of the questions – the data will be reliable, easy to access and update, and credible when used to put together arguments for additional resources or cooperation.

- *Accounts* – Financial information can be extremely useful to departments other than accounts, but few departments take the time to make full use of the information. Once armed with the questions you want answers to you will not only find it easier to identify relevant figures, you may even find your accounts department willing to cooperate with you and help you set up relevant analyses.

- *Public sources* – We have already looked at ways in which you can obtain and use data from public sources. The problem is often not one of where can you find the relevant data but what do you want to know? Most people lack the sort of questions you now have to hand.

Informal sources

- *Staff feedback* – Let your staff tell you what they encounter when dealing directly with suppliers and customers. While allowing them to express their feelings you will be able to gauge levels of satisfaction, problems and potential issues and begin to plan how you are going to address them. This feedback can form a good set of additional notes which will not be usable as research or as a measure but will help you gain depth of understanding to the other information you collect in a more structured way.
- *Own observations* – Add to the feedback you receive from your staff and colleagues by spending time with your customers and suppliers. Keep your own personal records to help you in your analysis and in your preparations for future meetings or communications.
- *Other* – Newsletters, brochures, web sites, press cuttings and other similar sources can be used to help you maintain an informal store of basic information on key players. Information of this kind can be helpful in a number of different situations.

ACTION BOX 8.6

Using the group selected in the previous Action Box collect relevant data for this group using existing and informal sources. Review the uses you can put this new information to.

Tables, charts, etc.

Here are some basic rules to help you get the most out of your data using tables, charts, and so on:

- *Time* – Always mark charts and tables with the time the data refer to. Try to compare results for periods that are comparable. It may be obvious that a week's sales data should not be compared to a month's but other comparisons could be just as misleading so be clear about what you are monitoring and how your time intervals affect what you are monitoring. If you are planning to compare figures over a set period (daily figures over the coming month, monthly figures across a year, etc.) make charts or tables that show the whole period for comparison and add figures to show changes or trends. Make the time element work for you. Remember that you usually need more than two results to identify a trend!

■ *Scales* – The classic pitfall is the use of inappropriate scales for graphs and charts. Changes in a graph should make things clearer so do not be tempted to magnify or minimize changes by changing scales. If you are looking for trends, you are unlikely to find them by exaggerating the fluctuations within the trend. Minimizing differences can be discouraging to staff who have worked hard to increase production or sales while exaggerated scales showing declines can badly demotivate staff. Think carefully about the uses of the graph or chart and about who will use them.

■ *Combinations and comparisons* – Do not try to make a chart or graph do too many jobs for you. Comparing several products or services may be an attractive idea but check to make sure the results can be understood and that you are comparing like with like. For example, if you wish to compare the performance of a high-volume item with that of a low-volume one over time you might find it difficult to compare their sales volumes. One solution might be to have a graph with two sales volume scales (on the right have the relevant scale for the high-volume items and on the left the low-volume scale) so that the variations can be shown together (see the examples in Figures 8.3 and 8.4). Alternatively you might be able to use percentage changes or percentages of total sales for the year.

■ *Display and share* – The measures you are gathering and monitoring need to be used as management tools. They need to be shared and understood by those involved in creating them and changing them. They also need to be part of the review process for them and for you with your manager. Selecting charts and tables for public display versus reports requires considerable thought. Ask yourself what will be positive motivators and what will be unhelpful or even oppressive. Make certain that if you are going to present data publicly it presents positive messages, involves people, relates to situations and figures that your staff can directly influence. Think of appropriate locations and vehicles for the figures. What can

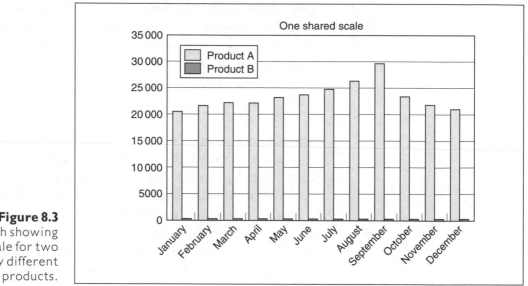

Figure 8.3
Graph showing
one scale for two
very different
products.

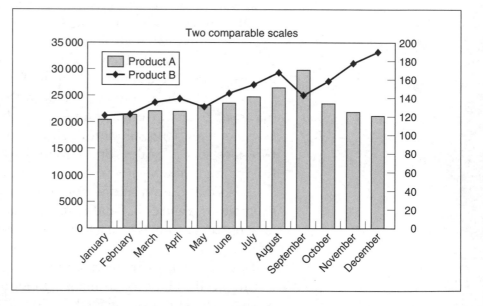

Figure 8.4
Graph showing
the same figures
using two scales.

go on the wall and which wall should you use? Can figures go on the notice board or in the newsletter? Could they go on the web site or departmental reports?

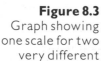

ACTION BOX 8.7

Use the new information you have on your customer group to put together a short presentation or report to your staff and/or selected colleagues.

HOW TO USE YOUR MEASURES

Finally, here are three important areas of use for the measuring and monitoring you will be doing.

Current position

Good managers will always be able to tell you the current position of their department and staff. Use your measures to help you do this. You should:

- *Monitor for performance* – Your figures will tell you which staff, departments and products or services are performing well at the moment, what people currently think of your products or services, which regions or outlets are doing well and so on. Keeping figures up to date and visible help you understand and manage things better and show people that you do know what is happening and why.

- *Monitor for position* – Measures tell you where you stand at the moment. If you know which part of the cycle you are on at any given time you can explain why figures are down without being defensive about it. Use your current versus past position to motivate and reward staff while seeking further support from superiors. Knowing how you compare with other departments, competitors or with the national situation is also important.

Future watching

What can your measures tell you about where you are going? Two important things to consider:

- *Monitor for trends* – Although this can be done by simply looking at the direction your graphs are taking it is not the only approach. Simple alternatives include: *percentage changes* showing percentage changes between each period; *indexed changes* comparing figures to an annual average; *same period last year* comparisons; *cumulative figures* showing how the figures are growing over time; *compared to target* either as a percentage or with target and actual on the same chart; *cumulative comparison* with target; *smoothed averages* (add the past three periods' figures together and divide by 3 and do this for all previous periods going back to the first three periods' figures and show as a graph) as smoothing can reduce the effect of small fluctuations and can show underlying trends. Whatever method you use, what you are looking for is the standard pattern you would expect based on seasonal or other patterns and the underlying trend indicating how well or badly you are doing.

■ *Monitor for warning signs* – The figures you collect will become familiar to you very quickly and you will begin to know what to expect based on past experience and on your knowledge of current events within your department, organization, and national or regional situation. Use this familiarity to help you develop a more sensitive approach to the information. Make connections between the informal comments you hear and the trends that are revealing themselves in the figures. You should be better able to anticipate changes, manage temporary problems and avoid potential disasters. The information will help you decide who should act (your staff, you, your boss?) as well as what you should do.

Actions

■ *Monitor for plans* – The measures you are making should become an integral part of your planning process. They should be able to tell you how, where and when to allocate resources most effectively, they should indicate problem areas that need resolving and enable you to make more measurable and timely objectives. If the data cannot help you in your planning work you need to plan to change or improve your measures.

■ *Monitor for rewards* – Many organizations use measures to help them provide incentives and reward achievements. Holiday and entertainment organizations frequently use customer satisfaction levels as part of their assessment and reward schemes for staff, customers on frequent usage or purchase schemes are rewarded based on measures of purchase, and discounts of all sorts can be based on similar measures. The measures you use may be on a very small or a very large scale but their impact can be as targeted or as general as you wish to make them.

ACTION BOX 8.8

Identify the data you currently use for the six areas above. Improve one aspect of each based on the notes in this section.

Conclusions

Measuring and monitoring are an integral part of the process of planning and implementing good customer relations. They span the full range of activities involved and provide important information to feed back into the planning and improvement processes as we will see in the following chapters.

Competence self-assessment

1 What are the five reasons why we measure the things we do? Give an example to illustrate each one.
2 What are the four general principles in measurement and why are they important?
3 Name three key aspects of a product/service you use that you know are measured regularly.
4 Identify four aspects of a process in your department that should be measured and monitored and explain why.
5 Identify one internal and one external partner you monitor on a regular basis and explain why you measure, what you measure and how you measure.
6 Describe three different types of measure you use to tell you how well you are serving your customers.
7 Name one formal and one informal source of information important to you and describe what they provide.
8 What do you need to monitor in order to be able to check your current and future position with regard to a key customer?

CHAPTER 9

Virtuous cycles

Use virtuous cycles to meet your customer's needs while securing the maximum benefit for the organization (meeting the organization's aims). Test each part of the plan and the whole plan against the VC rules. Are your plans sustainable, additive, positively dynamic, stable and integrated? E-commerce is a good example of this concept.

WHAT ARE VIRTUOUS CYCLES?

Basic concept

Our understanding of virtuous cycles has grown out of observation and research. Work in areas such as quality has shown us that some of the most effective routes to continuous improvement come from a cyclical process where needs are identified, improvements designed and planned, agreement is made and improvements are implemented, resulting in a review which feeds back into the whole process again. These feedback loops or cycles can be negative as well as positive and many situations of decline can be described using a negative feedback loop where the decline is incremental, feeding on itself.

The reason why virtuous cycles are desirable within management is their ability to generate regular or continuous improvement when started. Virtuous cycles create positive feedback generating incremental improvements. Part of management involves looking for and stopping negative cycles and either turning them into or replacing them with virtuous cycles. When making management improvements it is possible to address the outcome of negative cycles without removing them. In such cases we end up constantly dealing with the symptoms rather than the cause, hence, the importance of carrying out careful analysis and making full use of virtuous cycles.

What do they look like?

They are usually simple cause-and-effect loops such as the one in Figure 9.1 below.

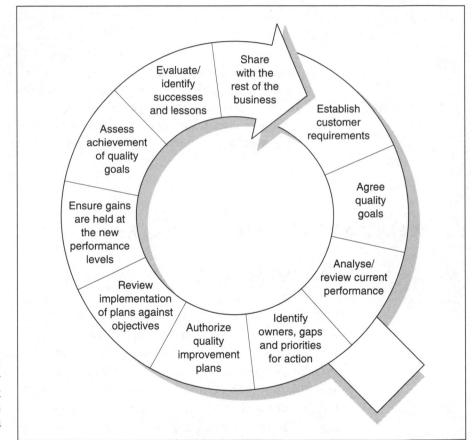

Figure 9.1
The quality improvement process as an example of a virtuous cycle.

It is clear from the diagram that the process is designed to feed back into itself with each link leading on to the next level of improvement.

There are a number of other examples where cycles within management are usually 'virtuous'. The budgeting process, for example, should be one such example with the work invested in producing the department's budgets help it to cost and evaluate each action against the resources available. These figures are then used to help manage the department's activities leading to a better understanding of what happens and why things happen during the year to cause the budgets to be the same or different from the agreed budget. These are then fed back into the design of the following year's budget. The outcome should reflect a set of positive changes and improvements that help make management in the following year better than the previous year.

All systems need to be monitored and managed properly and because of the special nature of feedback loops it is important to ensure that your monitoring is effective. Two problems that can occur from poor monitoring are a sudden and rapid decline when the loop becomes negative. This is caused by the additive nature of loops (see below). The other common problem is where a loop handles a problem too well and ends up exacerbating it. This happens either when the loop is placed in the wrong part of a process or when the problem is so efficiently dealt with it is allowed to grow.

An example of the second problem can help us understand more about cycles.

A rapidly growing insurance company encountered a problem with a small number of the applications it received. A small number of applicants made mistakes which delayed their applications significantly. To deal with this a small team was assigned to identify problem applications and deal with them directly. This team was effectively a loop created to solve a minor customer problem and it was seen as adding value in a customer-friendly way.

A couple of years later the company was taken over by a larger business and a review of performance took place. It found a significant amount of resources being spent on dealing with mistakes in application forms and, despite this, there was a large backlog of customers not being dealt with, long lead times for applications and business was being lost (along with considerable goodwill).

Analysis showed that the problem was not an over-zealous department handling incorrect applications. Instead it showed that the loop had been put in the wrong position. It was dealing with the symptom not the problem and its effectiveness had caused the problem to grow to enormous proportions.

The problem lay in the design of the form itself and in who was allowed to change the design. As the form changed it became harder to complete and less efficient at collecting relevant data. Instead of improving the form the team handling badly completed forms had been left to deal with the growing problem.

> By inserting a loop earlier to ensure that the forms were properly designed and met the needs of both the company and the customers using them, it was possible to eliminate most of the problems and, with proper systems in place to monitor any problems that arose, it was possible to keep them to the minimum.

Cycles are good at performing the task you design them for so it is important to use them for the correct purpose and monitor them carefully.

You can expect virtuous cycles to already exist within your organization because they are not an invention; they have been observed by people in a wide range of activities from economics and social science to ecology and geology. They are examples of how human beings design the things around them as well as how nature designs systems. They are convenient, efficient and successful and have always been a part of good management.

ACTION BOX 9.1

Identify a virtuous cycle in your current activities and map the various elements of the cycle out showing how it can be looped into a continuous cycle.

The five tests

Once you have discovered that some of the processes in your department are part of or make up what you believe to be virtuous cycles, how do you know you are right or that they are virtuous? In addition to being identifiable as cycles, processes described as virtuous cycles should also be the following:

- *Sustainable* – A process that feeds back on itself then stops is not sustainable. Either there is a link missing or it is a simple process. Do you need to make it cyclical? Does it need to be sustainable or is it simply a process required on a periodic basis? Virtuous cycles carry out a series of processes leading to the provision of new input to start the sequence of processes again.
- *Additive* – The output from the system or cycle should be measurably greater than the input. This is not always as obvious as it appears. Virtuous cycles designed to provide

support within a difficult work situation can appear to have little or no appreciable effect while contributing greatly in a number of ways. Examples like this can be found in professions where great stress occurs (in areas of the health service, for example) and where the cycle enables professionals to continue to operate effectively and where removal of the loop would result in high staff turnover and reduction in efficiency and effectiveness. Measuring the effect requires a clear understanding of what the cycle is doing.

- *Positively dynamic* – For the cycle to be virtuous it needs to be sustainable and additive in a positive way. Again, obvious, but only when the cycle is properly understood. The example of the cycle in the previous section was sustainable and additive, it appeared to be positively dynamic dealing with bigger and bigger problems as efficiently as any system could. However, it was not solving the problem. It was dynamic but you need a system overview to know whether its action is really positive, or just appears to be so.

- *Integrated* – Your virtuous cycles should not be operating outside the normal activities of your department. If you are managing such a cycle do you need to review the extent of your operations, are you doing another department's job or is it a partnership with one or more other departments?

- *Stable* – Systems can be both dynamic and stable. Stability in this context refers to the robustness of the system itself. If a virtuous cycle is doing its job and meets all of the other criteria but is still unstable, the probable reason is that the cycle is missing a link or has extraneous functions creating instability within the cycle. By tracing the processes step by step it should become obvious where the problem lies. A good example of this problem is where the feedback part of the cycle is a link between departments where a difference in authority or operational status occurs. In such cases the feedback of problems is delivered by a junior manager or clerk to a senior manager in another department or from a clerical staff member to technical specialists.

ACTION BOX 9.2

Apply the five-point test to your cycle and see how you can improve and develop it. What is missing or needs to be clarified to improve the cycle?

From our description so far, it is clear that if you want to develop and use virtuous cycles you will need to be able to understand and analyse them in some detail. Once you can do this you can build them and the analysis they bring into your planning process. The following sections help you look at these cycles in more detail.

A CLOSER LOOK AT CYCLES

Managers need to be able to review and improve different aspects of their department's work. When looking at how to use virtuous cycles you can use an established set of sequences to initiate improvements to relationships as well as processes.

Start with the agreed task

Let us use an example to help explain the process. The manager of a confectionery manufacturer's quality control laboratory is responsible for ensuring the quality of all the ingredients, manufactured products and wrappings/packaging used by the manufacturer. Each department that relies on the quality control laboratory works with the manager to ensure that materials are available for testing at the appropriate times, and that the staff employed to carry out sampling collect materials for testing, after which the manager delivers reports on their quality.

At each stage, the timing is critical to ensure that the quality does not drop and that products are manufactured on time as well as to standard.

One task for the manager is to test liquid glucose to ensure it is of the appropriate quality for the different manufacturing processes. Timing has always been a problem in this area and so the manager set out to see what she could do to improve things.

The task as defined by her was to ensure that all glucose delivered was tested and assured to the appropriate standard. The problem was that the glucose deliveries happened at times based on the 'just in time' principle which meant that orders were placed close to the time when they were needed and the supplier delivered within a given time. The glucose was delivered in large tankers and needed to be pumped into the special hoppers as quickly as possible after the tanker's arrival. There were three tests required on the glucose; one could be completed in less than half an hour but the others could take much longer. The manager's predecessor had compromised on the testing by conducting the shortest test immediately the tanker arrived, and conducted the other tests after delivery based on the calculated risk that if the glucose passed the short test it had a very high probability of passing the other tests. He had invested in the latest equipment to ensure speedy analysis and had located the equipment in a small room now known as the Glucose Lab simply for this test.

Variations in quality were becoming significant in the supplies used by the company as suppliers changed their sources and processes, and the current manager was now concerned about this risk.

Her initial attempt at improving the process involved meeting with the managers of the different departments using the raw materials to find out how she could work with them to improve things. No one wanted to increase lead times to allow her to carry out the longer tests and the costs would rise significantly if they kept tankers waiting to deliver glucose. Longer lead times affected the efficiency of the manufacturing process which, in turn, increased costs. They wanted her to speed up the analysis processes but she had been working on this and had not found a solution yet.

Next she went to the buyers – if the manufacturing departments could not help, could the people who bought the supplies? Traditionally there were few direct links between the quality control laboratory and the buyers as they worked with the manufacturing departments and it was manufacturing who provided samples of materials from new or potential suppliers and worked with the buyers on the results. This was a new approach.

They did not seem to be able to help at first. They felt that she was questioning their ability to buy suitable quality materials and pointed out the very low incidence of problems in this area. It took some time to work around this initial attitude but eventually it became clear that it was in the buyers' interests to help find a solution to the problem.

Timing was a known and agreed part of the equation and the suppliers were rotated based on a mixture of current market prices and the need to balance use of different suppliers, but sources could be identified prior to delivery. Nothing could be done to improve access to materials prior to their delivery, however, as the next order would result in a tanker being loaded and transported to the factory immediately. Biking samples in advance would not produce much of an advantage.

With the buyers' agreement, the manager contacted each of the suppliers in turn and discovered that each had their own quality control laboratory (not a surprise to her) and that they all carried out the same tests as she did prior to the glucose being stored in hoppers ready for distribution. With only minor problems to solve it was possible to agree that these laboratories would fax her details of their tests on the batches being sent by their companies to her factory. After a few blind tests she was able to ascertain how closely her tests and theirs correlated. She was then able to carry out the quick test, compare it with the results from the supplier's laboratory and guarantee the quality of the materials.

Three things to note

- First, she had solved the problem by looking beyond the assumed area of the process in question.
- Second, she had re-examined her role and position within the organization and adjusted it without causing any conflict or problems despite initial concerns.
- Third, she had built new relationships and developed partnerships in order to solve the problem.

The results included:

- Better testing and improved services to her clients.
- Better relationships with her clients and with other internal departments.
- New and valuable relations with other important and hitherto unused partners in the process.
- Improved basis for negotiation between suppliers and buyers.
- Quality control brought into the buyer–supplier loop.
- Continuous quality monitoring and resulting improvements in quality as well as relations.

The original loop had been extended from an exchange between the quality control laboratory with the inclusion of a new small laboratory but this had reduced the effects of the problem rather than solving them. The solution was not part of the whole process. It had no means by which developments and continuous improvements could be found and introduced into the process.

The final loop was cyclical and met the other requirements being sustainable, additive, stable and integrated. The loop had moved out to address the real problem in a way that involved not only a solution but a process that offered opportunities for continuous improvement at a number of levels. It was a virtuous cycle of improvement.

> **ACTION BOX 9.3**
>
> Identify a loop you might improve by changing where it is placed or its focus. Would adding additional stages or incorporating another process transform it?

BALANCING INPUTS AND OUTPUTS

We have already identified that virtuous cycles add value. What are these cycles like in more detail? Let us review what *we* put into these cycles.

Outward – expenditures

What do you contribute as the cycle progresses towards the customer?

- *Resources* – How much do you invest in making the cycle happen, how much do you contribute in your own and staff time, energies and other measures of resources? Do you contribute to all or just some stages and who/which other departments contribute, too?
- *Your products/services* – This may appear obvious at first but consider what you have learned about your products/services and answer this by identifying what is entailed when you provide your products or services (at the Core, Tangible and Augmented levels as well as along the route to your customers). Which, if any, of these elements are part of the cycle you are considering?
- *Basic support* – Alongside the product/service you provide essential support. Is this a cycle that is built around providing or linked with this sort of support?
- *Added value* – Where are elements of added value put into the cycle and what does that cost in time, effort and resources? Where do these come from and who are they accountable to?

What else can you identify as costs or expenditure invested in the cycle by you, your department or organization? What goes into making the cycle work – you need to know in order to assess the benefits accruing from the cycle. Try to separate out one-off costs and occasional and continuous costs, as the cycle should repeat itself and some initial costs should be minimized once things are up and running (good examples of this might be initial training costs or software/set-up costs).

Inward – incomes

This is the other side of the balance or scales. What comes from having the cycle, and how 'virtuous' is it?

- *Custom* – Gaining custom from individuals or organizations may be considered as the key gain of any process.
- *Income* – Growing from *custom* is income whether it is wholly financial or measured partly or fully in other ways. How you identify and measure your income from custom will be a crucial element in your assessment of the cycle you are examining. Explore all aspects of what you gain through your exchanges with customers – the benefits accruing to you as a result of what your customers get at each level in the products/services you provide will be important in this exploration of cycles.
- *Repeat custom* – As well as an outcome of a successful set of processes it is also a measurable benefit (especially when set against the cost of trying to find brand new customers). Every customer retained and nurtured yields a higher return than a new customer and usually does (or should do) so more than once.
- *Benefits* – Other measurable benefits or outcomes might include internal rewards for improved relationships with customers, attraction of additional resources as a result of the cycle's success, and so on.

Once you have identified all of the costs and benefits involved in the cycle you are looking at, take the time to list them and compare what has gone in and what is coming out of the sequence of processes. This will help you have a much clearer idea of the whole cycle and highlight any problems, missing links or needed improvements as well as demonstrate the value of the cycle. Figure 9.2 illustrates the layout of a simple table that will help you carry out this task.

Out	In
Details and costs expenditure	**Details and value of income benefits**
Total out =	**Total in =**

Figure 9.2
Table to weigh the balance between outputs and inputs in a cycle.

> **ACTION BOX 9.4**
>
> Use the table in Figure 9.2 to help you review the processes within a cycle currently active within your department. How positive is the cycle and where could improvements or changes increase its cycle of improvement?

NEGATIVE INFLUENCES

These are the possible constraints faced by existing and new virtuous cycles. They also apply to the planning process as a whole and will be used again in Chapter 10. This is a general list of influences to consider and therefore not all will apply in every case.

Constraints

- *Physical* – Is what you propose actually realistic, can it be done and continue to be done?
- *Resources* – What do you need to make it happen? Do you have enough people, materials, resources to make it possible or worthwhile?
- *Cost* – Does the cost outweigh the benefits (remember the balancing you have to do in your assessment)?
- *Internal needs and structures* – Are the internal needs met and can the structures be used or is the cycle working against rather than with them? Is it going to have a positive effect on them?
- *Customer needs* – Will it help you to meet your customers' needs (assuming that is what you are trying to do) or is it going to be a disadvantage?

Competition

Competitive activity – Is this a diversion and are you spending resources and energies countering competitor activities that would be better spent serving customers? Is the competitor setting the agenda? If the answer is 'yes' is it:

- A *defensive response?* – Not designed to improve but simply to defend your current position.
- An *aggressive response?* – Designed to attack but without clear positive outcome for your product/service or customers.

Environment

- *Noise* – Noise distorts understanding and can stop you from producing well thought out responses to problems. Good research and market intelligence and refusing to simply react without analysing situations will help you avoid the effects of 'environmental noise'.
- *Social* – How acceptable are your solutions in the context of who your customers are and how they live and operate? Do they solve your problems without taking customers and the social context into account?
- *Legal* – Always be clear about both general legal issues and contractual ones.
- *Political/cultural* – Important regional, national and international as well as cultural differences will affect how your solutions to problems are accepted.

ACTION BOX 9.5

List the key negative influences you can identify in a current cycle and explore ways in which you could transform these or reduce their negative effects.

POSITIVE ASPECTS

When assessing your activities generally, as well as in the context of virtuous cycles, you are advised to examine the positive as well as the negative aspects of your activities. These should be considered within the process as well as in terms of the outcomes. Results may be important but excellent results can be quickly negated if the price paid for the results is high. Best not to aim for a situation where your situation is summed up by the statement, 'I have the best products in the world but all of my suppliers and customers hate me'.

What should you be looking for? This is a short survey of positive aspects to consider.

Knowledge

- *Knowing needs* – Both learning more about them through the process and responding to them in a manner that demonstrates your understanding. Can your customers see this, too?
- *Knowing value* – As with needs, how does it add to your understanding of the value exchanges in the process, how does it add value and can customers see the difference?
- *Quality* – The third facet of knowledge is learning about quality, acting on quality and delivering improvements in quality in a clear way.

Communications

- *Reaching customers* – How is it connecting with and affecting your customers?
- *Developing dialogue* – Is it opening channels for your customers to help you improve your provision to them? Is it helping you exchange ideas, opening channels for you respond to what they are saying to you?
- *Responding to them* – How is it responding to your customers? What are you doing about what they say, want, feel and so on?
- *Tone of voice* – Is it positively affecting the way you talk to them?
- *Content* – Is it changing what you say to them, what you do for them, what you are planning for the future, what you are saying to the other players involved in the process, and so on?

Innovation

The lifeblood of much competitive advantage, improvements and developments is innovation. Often, small innovations in a number of areas can transform any activity in a less disruptive, more effective way than single, massive innovations. What can your processes and cycles do to find and add those small innovations as well as point to larger improvements?

Profit

Do not forget to revisit this in each review or evaluation. Profit, we have shown, is both directly and indirectly financially measured. Freeing staff time, increasing productivity, increasing turnover, improving quality and reducing costs are profit contributors. How do your activities bring these about and how well do they do this?

ACTION BOX 9.6

Using the same cycle as in Action Box 9.5 add a list of positive influences and explore how you could exploit them further.

YOU, YOUR CUSTOMERS AND VIRTUOUS CYCLES

The beginning of this chapter used a quality-improvement cycle as an example of a virtuous cycle. Here are two further examples of virtuous cycles focused on managing to meet customer needs.

Organizational balance

Planning to improve your performance in meeting customer needs requires that you find a balance between serving internal and external needs. Use this virtuous cycle to help you do your planning.

Keeping informed

Who do you need to keep informed? Staff need to know even if they are not directly involved in an activity; your bosses and fellow managers may need to know either out of courtesy, for management reasons or as part of the process of sharing information. Customers and suppliers may also need to be informed of what is happening. Make certain you know who should be kept informed, how much you

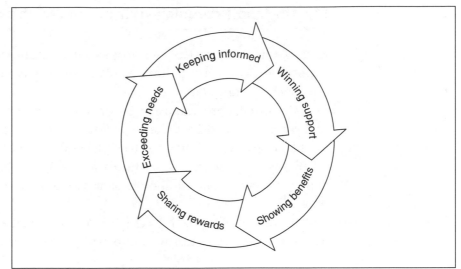

Figure 9.3
Cycle of
improvement.

need to tell them and why. Changes in personnel and developments in your activities should prompt you to inform.

Winning support

Success through cooperation and support is usually more stable and long-lasting. Build into your plans sufficient time and effort to ensure you win support from those you have informed. Those providing support may expect to share in the benefits but their support reduces risk and increases chances of success.

Showing benefits

All players need to know how well things are going and what the results of activities and efforts are − if you invest in something you want to know the outcome. Communication does not stop when you tell people what you are going to do − tell them how successful it was.

Sharing rewards

Share the rewards with your department − every success you share adds to your success while rewarding and motivating your staff. Managers never lose when they share success with their staff. Then share success with those whose support you enjoyed for the same reasons. Let them know they played a part, too, and they will continue to invest in your activities.

Meeting and exceeding your organization's needs

Part of this is related to the targets set by the organization and the expectations of your customers. Part of this is related to how you approach the targets.

If the targets are impossible to achieve there is something wrong and you need to address that problem before acting on them. Targets are like objectives, they need to be SMART (see Chapter 5, page 97). Your objective should be to find ways of exceeding the targets and expectations but targets should be reasonable and objectives need to be achievable.

Adopting an approach based on this cycle helps you reach a point where incremental improvements will exceed targets.

ACTION BOX 9.7

Try developing your own cycle of improvement for an area of responsibility you wish to improve. Use your outline and notes as the basis for a meeting with key players in this area and facilitate the meeting to use their input to develop, improve and jointly implement the cycle.

You and your department

Monitor your customer-centred projects in a positive way using a virtuous cycle like the one below in Figure 9.4.

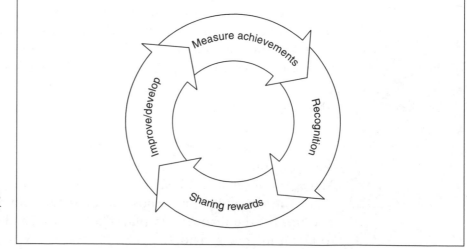

Figure 9.4
Cycle of incremental improvement.

Achievements

Monitor progress and measure achievements as the project is being carried out. Identify the source and value of achievements within the project. This will help you spread good practice as well as praise.

Recognition

Give recognition for achievements. Praise and encouragement are valuable aspects of management but they should be related to actual performance and actions. Monitoring and measuring allows you to know where improvements lie as well as where extra effort has been made. Showing you have seen and are recognizing these encourages improved performance and increases confidence and trust in your staff and colleagues.

Rewards

Rewards should be varied and shared. Alongside personal recognition of achievement goes public recognition within the group and organization using meetings, notice boards and newsletters as well as reports and personal references to your own and other managers. Rewards also include financial and resource-based awards and bonuses, allocation of equipment and staff time, training and other relevant provision.

Improving and developing

Feed the best practice, good performance and improvements in approach or technique into the rest of your department's work and see where it can be used to improve other areas of the organization's activities. Each time new improvements are fed back into the system it gives you and your co-workers the opportunity to improve on them. This is the key to making virtuous cycles work for you.

ACTION BOX 9.8

Use this cycle as a model to help you develop a service to one of your internal customers. Involve both your staff and representatives from your internal customers in the final development and implementation process.

VIRTUOUS CYCLES – AN EXAMPLE IN E-COMMERCE

We have outlined how new technology is affecting customer relations in earlier chapters. One aspect of this new technological change is described by the term E-Commerce.

E-Commerce provides managers in a number of sectors with the opportunity to develop customer-facing systems with the classic elements of a virtuous cycle built into many of its processes.

These can be summarized as follows.

The communications cycles

Web sites can be used to build communications and exchanges by providing detailed and accessible information on products or services, on the organization, on the uses or processes surrounding the products/services and on user comments and advice. It can also provide interactive question and answer or problem-solving services and an opportunity for current and past users to exchange inform-ation, views and advice.

The design of the web site therefore needs to allow the most rele-vant and useful elements to be available and accessible in easy and user-friendly forms. The design then facilitates a user or customer-based communications process where customers use the site to inform themselves and share information which you, the provider, can use to help you develop and improve your provision of products or services. The web site, by performing these functions, also adds value to the customer's experience and improves their view of you.

The cycles of improvement based on the provision and facilitation of customer information are clear.

Linked to the provision of information are the opportunities for the customer to sample, test and buy your products and services either via retail outlets pointed to from the site or directly through the site. Each time customers access and use the site you have poten-tial opportunities to communicate with them and gather information about them. The most powerful gathering processes occur when the customer opts to provide you with data when communicating with you and other customers and when buying or requesting things from you. The buying element allows you to add further value and cred-ibility through ensuring that the transaction is secure and working efficiently. You obtain custom, income and information in a quick and easily usable form and you provide fast and easy-to-use services in return. The exchange can only be marred if your security is poor or you have not developed a delivery system equal to the other parts of the E-Commerce process. Delivery should be fast, efficient and reliable if you are intending to embark on the E-Commerce route.

Again the cycles are both clear and meet the requirements necessary for them to be virtuous.

Finally, the broader communications aspects of the system also support the virtuous nature of the whole process. Web sites are easy to maintain and service and provide an open-access route for customers across the world. Web addresses are expected to be an integral part of all communications these days and a significant part of the promotion of most is based on a combination of ensuring your site is included in the results of all leading search engines when key words are used in their searches. Word of mouth is also the other key method of exchange and promotion for sites. The provision of an element of E-Commerce within your customer communications programme serves each aspect of the relationship you have and wish to develop with your customers and meets a key need they expect you to be able to meet. It provides a set of important and valuable new cycles that sit alongside existing programmes adding value and support in ways that are often defined and led by customers rather than by you. This adds to their value and to their efficiency.

Competence self assessment

1 Describe what a virtuous cycle is in your own words.
2 What are the five tests for a virtuous cycle?
3 What do you have to balance in a virtuous cycle and why is balance so important?
4 Identify four key positive and negative influences affecting a virtuous cycle you are involved in at work.
5 What are the five key elements in the cycle of improvement and how do they help organizational balance?
6 List the four stages in the cycle used to monitor and improve customer-centred projects.
7 How can E-Commerce add new cycles to your activities with customers?

CHAPTER 10

Revisiting your plans

Having plans is not the same as putting plans into action. Meeting customer needs will require managing activities internally as well as externally placed. While ensuring staff play their part some plans may require compliance and cooperation with other departments. Plans may also involve the management or cooperation with others including external suppliers, those on delivery or supply chains and external agencies providing marketing related services.

Planning is the core activity of managers. It is how we know what we are doing and why, it is about how we do what we have to do, who we do it with and for, and it is about how we know we have done the right thing, done it properly and achieved our goals. The planning process should be a classic virtuous cycle that goes as follows:

Summarize where you are now, what your resources are and what you are required to do; make a proper *assessment* of these and *develop your ideas* of where you could go from here; identify and frame your *objectives* for change and improvement as well as maintenance; prepare *strategies* or guidelines for the processes and activities you will need to perform in order to meet these new objectives; write your *operating plan* along with assessments and reviews; *do it* (carry out your plans); take the *results* including *assessments* and *reviews* and *feed them back* into the start of a new planning phase; *summarize* where you are now, and so on.

Planning is also a valuable tool to help you review what you have learned and direct it towards key areas in your management activities. As this book focuses on meeting customer needs we will use that focus to help you review and plan improvements in that area. However, the same approach can be used in many other areas of the management process. Take advantage of them wherever you find them useful.

The beginning of the planning process is traditionally centred on carrying out an audit. The early part of this book helped the reader prepare most of the ingredients of a suitable audit and we will use these to help you prepare a new, or review your existing, plan.

AUDIT

To audit is to review and take everything relevant into account. It is the point in the planning process where you have the opportunity to look at everything within the work you are doing and look out at everything that affects what you are doing.

What to include

The checklist for an audit tends to be very long and you may find that not all of it is relevant to your circumstances. However, it is worth working your way through the checklist and where the individual areas do not appear relevant ask yourself why it is not relevant, and also what aspect of the area might be relevant or if there is an equivalent area that is relevant.

Your next task is then to gather information on each area and assemble it together to help you make sense of your current position.

Here is a checklist for an audit you can use. The list includes all of the areas covered in the previous chapters of this book and if you have been following the Activity Boxes so far you will already have most of the information required to complete your own audit.

Collect all of the information you can for this phase. The more you know about your current position the better your position when it comes to making decisions and the stronger your arguments for adopting particular approaches, strategies or for claiming resources. Expect those who manage you to have more and better information than you have and welcome any support, advice and information they can provide you with during the planning process.

ACTION BOX 10.1

Using your current departmental plans review the audit using the checklist above and if sections are missing you feel should be there, or if there is no audit in the plan, add what you believe to be necessary to provide proper background information for the plan.

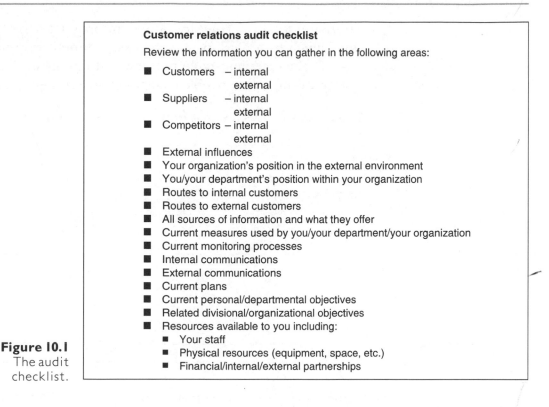

Customer relations audit checklist

Review the information you can gather in the following areas:

- Customers – internal
  external
- Suppliers – internal
  external
- Competitors – internal
  external
- External influences
- Your organization's position in the external environment
- You/your department's position within your organization
- Routes to internal customers
- Routes to external customers
- All sources of information and what they offer
- Current measures used by you/your department/your organization
- Current monitoring processes
- Internal communications
- External communications
- Current plans
- Current personal/departmental objectives
- Related divisional/organizational objectives
- Resources available to you including:
  - Your staff
  - Physical resources (equipment, space, etc.)
  - Financial/internal/external partnerships

Figure 10.1
The audit checklist.

MAKING SENSE OF THINGS

There are a number of simple techniques you can use to help you make sense of the information you have gathered. Some of them should already be familiar to you.

One of the most commonly used, and one we recommend for this stage of the process, is the SWOT analysis. The four letters refer to Strengths, Weaknesses, Opportunities and Threats.

Strengths usually refer to *internal* factors such as product or service quality, lower costs than your competitors, effective and well-trained sales people, etc.

Weaknesses also tend to be *internal* factors such as small size compared to your major competitors, limited communications budget, and so on.

Opportunities are usually derived from *external* factors such as new export market opportunities now opened to you, the financial difficulties of a major competitor or a strike in their factory, etc.

Threats are usually *external* in nature and may take the form of the launch of a new and unexpected competitor product or service, the emergence of a new low-cost import or the uncertainty arising from possible changes in government policy.

The SWOT analysis uses a set of four quadrants as illustrated below:

Strengths	Opportunities
Weaknesses	Threats

Figure 10.2
The SWOT chart.

You use these to list the factors from your audit according to how you assess them. In addition to performing a general SWOT to give yourself an overview of your current position you can also use it to focus on an aspect of your activities and resources. SWOT analyses can be carried out on your communications, your products/services, your staff or department as a whole, and you can even carry out one on your own circumstances.

The simplicity of the SWOT can be a trap. Be careful of how you use this tool.

Do not assume that the number of factors in any given quadrant is all you need to know. A company can have ten strengths and only one weakness but if the weakness is vitally important (for example the company is making a steady loss) it may outweigh all ten of the strengths together.

Do not assume that the position of any factor is necessarily permanent. The analysis is designed to show you the areas you need to address and the perspective to help you change things.

Factors can be placed in two squares at the same time – for example, an organization's high profile and charismatic chief executive can be seen as both a strength and a weakness at the same time and the financial difficulties of a key competitor can be seen as both an opportunity and a threat.

Use the SWOT analysis to help you identify the changes and developments you will need to include in your next plan. The SWOT provides the overview of your current position and is there to help you see where you are doing well and how to turn the negative into the positive. So, *weaknesses can be turned into strengths and threats into opportunities*.

SWOT analyses can be useful as a tool for you to use on your own or in meetings with staff or colleagues. Working together to compile a SWOT can open up areas of discussion, bring new insights into the team and help share the discovery, development and implementation of new ideas and solutions across the team or between departments.

ACTION BOX 10.2

Identify an area of importance to you and your department and conduct your own SWOT analysis on it. Facilitate a departmental meeting where your staff can compile and share a SWOT analysis of the same area.

THE 'BIG PICTURE' BOX

There are basic questions you need to ask once you have explored the SWOT. You might want to ask yourself what your position is like generally. Can you step back and see how you and your department fits in with everything else? You have been working on aspects of this (the route to customers, for example) but can you get a feel for the even bigger picture? To do this you have to consider the big picture presented by all of the information you have.

Business gurus have called the ability to step back and look at this as 'helicoptering' – as if you sit in a helicopter and rise above everything so that you can look down and see what it looks like as a whole. You can imagine you and your department in the centre and see how things radiate out from you. You are the centre of it all; how close are the customers, the other players, how small or big are you in the scheme of things? The idea is not to demonstrate how important or insignificant you are compared to the rest of the world but to see how things fit together and why different aspects hold the importance they do.

If you find this hard to do or you want another more direct approach, review the results of the Audit and SWOT using the following questions and matrix.

Achieved? – What proportion of your required or expected work have you and your department completed? What could you not do or cannot do yet and why? Divide everything into required and done, required and yet to do and required but not possible. Try to get a fix on what the last year has been and what you and your department have really achieved.

Exceeded? – Where have you and your department exceeded targets, expectations or requirements? Look at these and split into important or valuable, nice to have or useful but not really essential and the icing on the cake but not really of great use, value or importance. Try to measure where the real successes were in the last year.

Could do better? – Be honest and candid with yourself (you need not share this with your boss – this is to help you do better) and review the activities of you and your department. Where do you need to introduce improvements, where did things fall short of expected or required levels, where could you and your department have done better? You can and should write down why as well and how you might be able to change things but start here by noting the areas of poor or low performance, the just misses, failures and so on. No system is perfect and if you cannot find these one of your failures might be that you have not reviewed everything you need to or you are not being honest or sufficiently critical.

Missing? – What have you not done that should have been done, what has become obvious or conspicuous by its absence, what are your competitors doing that you should be doing too, what do your customers, suppliers or bosses want that you need to put in your plans for next year? The current situation will always be mapped around some empty spaces and you should look at them before making your plans.

Changes where and why? – You can now see what could be or needs to be changed and can reason why the changes are needed. List them along with what the changes should achieve and who will benefit from them. What is new on your horizon and who is initiating it?

To help you sort this out use the following matrix. Which quadrants do you use? Most of the things you and your department do should end up in the bottom left-hand box with a few spread between the other three. The bias towards any given box tells you something useful about your current and future position.

As stated, the bulk in 'No change' should denote a stable situation.

Heavy bias towards 'Remove' could denote a department in decline unless it is balanced with a number of things in the 'New' box.

Heavy bias towards 'New' denotes a department in transition if linked with corresponding items in 'Change' or 'Remove' boxes. Otherwise it may be expanding.

Heavy bias towards 'Change' usually denotes a department in transition.

You need to look at the pattern to decide what your matrix means.

Change	New
No change	Remove

Figure 10.3
The 'big picture'
box.

ACTION BOX 10.3

Use the same details as in Action Box 10.2 and apply the 'big picture' box approach. Compare the outcomes.

PRIORITIES

The classic problem faced by managers when asked to prioritize is expressed as follows:

> 'Prioritize? Of course I do! *Everything* is high priority and that's my problem.'

Priorities are value judgements so you have to have a set of values to make the judgements. Here are some approaches you might consider.

Whose priorities?

All managers have to balance their needs with those of other players within their scope of activities. Decide whose needs and interests you are serving and review your activities against these groups. You should have enough information to help you do this but the exercise is also a useful way of double-checking the needs and views of certain groups. Once you have put down your idea of how things are use it to discuss priorities with key staff and as a prompt when sounding out your boss or other players.

Start by compiling a list of your current activities and placing them in the left-hand column of a table. Then add as many other columns as required for the different groups you serve. Possible columns might be A = internal customers, B = external customers, C = internal suppliers, D = external suppliers, E = stakeholders, F = your boss, G = your organization or division.

Your activities	A	B	C	D	E	F	G

Figure 10.4
The priority table.

Consider each activity in turn and place a tick in each column where an activity is relevant or important to a player. Once you have identified all of the activities and who you think needs and benefits from them try to rank them first by deciding the most important to least important activity with regards to you and your department. Then do the same for each of the players. As a guide 10 = top priority and 1 is the lowest priority. You can now see where conflicts can occur and where the issue of balancing your activities and relationships will need attention. Areas where everyone shares the same high or low priority will help you make some of those difficult decisions in your plans and will be useful while planning negotiations with your boss and other players.

ACTION BOX 10.4

Use the above analysis and incorporate it in your Action Box notes.

Other ranking approaches

For simple choices it is possible to rank actions or activities according to the level of their importance as follows:

Need to do – You have no choice and the priority, need, requirement is clear. These are the highest priority elements.

Best value – If you want to exceed expectations, add value or extend your department's achievements or improve already good experiences, etc., do this. Although they may be attractive they are at medium priority level.

Bonus items – Nice to have or do, attractive but their additional contribution does not justify even medium priority level status.

Using this simplified ranking system you divide your current or planned activities into three simple but practical groups or levels.

Other things to consider

We have used mapping techniques throughout this book to help us compare different values. This approach can be used to help you prioritize your activities (or objectives).

Here are four simple applications of this approach to help you sort out priorities and plan better.

The cost/priority box

Figure 10.5 illustrates this. Compare how much your activity/project/objective costs against the priority it enjoys.

If it is low cost and high priority the issue is simply *when* should you do it? Get it done! If it is high priority and high cost you need to be sure you have the funds to do it because it will need to be done. If it is low cost and low priority you might ask yourself can I fit it in this time around and if so, when? If it is low priority and high cost you need to ask hard questions about it. Why is it so costly and is it worth doing? Is it low priority because it has always demanded a high price to do?

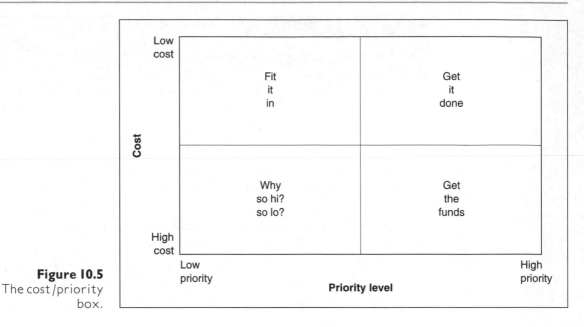

Figure 10.5
The cost/priority
box.

What happens if you lower the cost or if something changes to raise its priority?

The priority box

This helps you decide how to balance priorities. The priorities you wish to compare may change but try to keep the department's on one axis and compare them with another player's priorities.

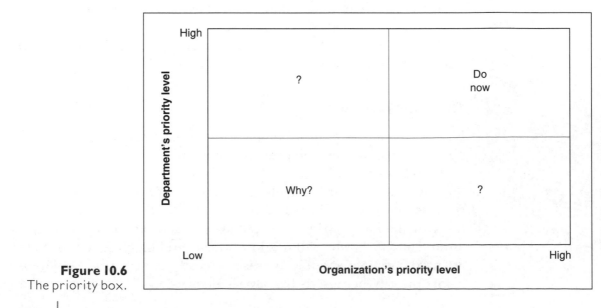

Figure 10.6
The priority box.

In this example, the question marks are the pivotal points. High priority for both parties gives you a clear signal – do it! Low priority for both leads you to ask why you have this activity or objective in the first place – it may be a priority from elsewhere. The two question marks are areas where balance will be required. The decisions you make here determine how you balance the priorities for your department with external priorities (in this case the organization's).

The value box

This can be used as a tool to compare the value of an activity to you against the value to your customer but, again, you can vary the players to help you make sense of an issue or problem. Here we have given the boxes a score for two reasons. First, in order to help with the following box and, more importantly, to demonstrate that this is another area where the balancing act must be faced. High value for both parties adds considerably to the importance of the activity while low value for both parties reduces it. The decisions are going to be made in the two boxes scoring 2 as here you will be either making a conscious decision that one or other party takes precedence or that some other factor needs to be considered before the decision can be made.

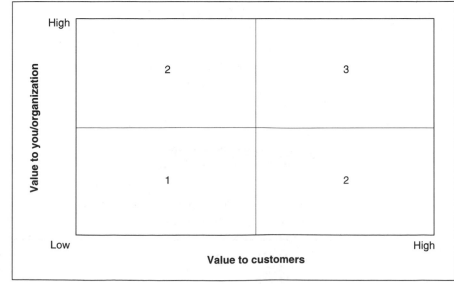

Figure 10.7
The value box.

The ease/value box

The final example in this section demonstrates how the box can be used to sort out activities or objectives based on how easy they are to do versus their value scores from the previous box exercise.

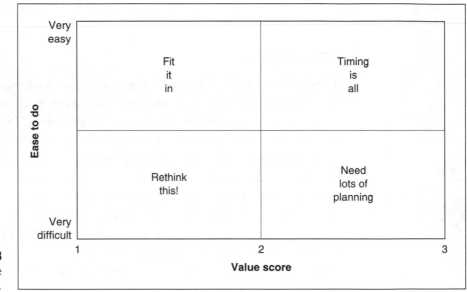

Figure 10.8
The ease/value
box.

If it is easy and scores a high value the case for doing it is so strong your problem is to decide the best time to do it (or start doing it). If it is easy to do but not enormously high value, can you fit it in? This will be determined by other things but may tip the balance if the score is 2 rather than 1. If it is high value but difficult to do you will have to consider how you do it, what you need to get it done, and so on. Planning is essential. However, if the cost is high and the value low the case is strong for you to rethink it or put it to one side and let other things take priority.

ACTION BOX 10.5

Using your department's current objectives, experiment with the approaches above to see how these might change your views of priorities and influence your future plans.

AIMS AND OBJECTIVES

We have covered what objectives are and how to set them in earlier chapters. Here we need to remind you to test them against the SMART objectives test and use the earlier sections of this chapter to help you prioritize and test your objectives.

The aims set by you or for you and stated in your plans are the starting point for the whole of your plans and activities. The aims state the purposes and outcomes of you and your department's activities. They should be clear, simple and encompassing.

When you are assessing your objectives and deciding things like priorities, targets, etc., each and every one should fit within the aims set for you. So, as a process for setting objectives, you should ensure that the objectives you identify and detail cover the aims you have. Then, as a double check, you need to revisit your aims with your objectives and ensure that you have covered what you are committed to in your aims through your objectives. Discrepancies, omissions and biases need to be addressed before you can be sure that the plans you are making are sufficient for your needs as a manager.

Plans

Plans are working documents and you will revisit and review them all the way through their period of implementation. New plans grow out of old ones and depend on the knowledge and understanding experience brings.

The following is designed to help you develop, revisit and review your plans.

Putting things together

In Chapter 5 we outlined what plans should do. Here is an expanded version of this list. Plans should:

- Address the relevant issues – will you meet and exceed your customer's expectations?
- Be practical and achievable – are you setting yourself up to fail? Will you promise your customers things you cannot deliver?

- Contain clearly defined objectives.
- Have strategies that can be implemented.
- Be flexible recognizing the effects of changes, failures and successes.
- Be accessible – who is it going to affect and how do you share it with them?
- Be tools that can be up-dated, revised and incorporated into other plans.
- Be accurate records of a situation at a particular point in time showing how you and your colleagues reacted to the situation.
- Contain accurate timings, costings and other action-based details.
- Contain accurate and reliable analyses.
- Be flexible working documents that really are used.
- Have a built-in recognition of success or failure (incrementally or recognizing degrees of success).
- Have progress built into them.
- Contain triggers for starting the planning process again if there is not already an on-going process in place (see virtuous cycles).
- Contain all of the relevant processes needed to implement each strategy.
- Include contingency plans.
- Have measurable outcomes.
- Contain processes to monitor progress and measure outcomes.

This is a fairly comprehensive list. It covers most eventualities and can be used as the starting point. From it develop your own checklist for use in your planning, changing and adding points where necessary. Planning needs to be a continuous learning process building on past work.

Application

Plans will not work if you do not apply them.

Making the written word come alive involves committing yourself and your team to the contents of the plan. Here are some guidelines to help you.

Setting your course

Gantt charts and other visual tools of management are helpful (see earlier chapters). You should have a clear understanding of when each part of the plan needs to be carried out, where, by whom and with what support. Before you can manage the process you need to understand it fully and share that with the others involved.

Making things happen

Four things help make things happen and make them work smoothly:

- *Sharing responsibility* – Usually you cannot do everything and are not expected to. Who will you share responsibility with, which staff and other players will be working directly with you? How are you going to manage their work and how are they going to have access to you?
- *Involving others* – Other departments may be involved on projects in your plan. They may be suppliers or internal customers or sharing in the flow of tasks within the larger project. How are you going to facilitate their cooperation and how will you ensure the coordination of efforts, etc?
- *Monitoring* – This is where monitoring becomes critical. How will you know what is going well and what is going wrong, how will you know when the work is finished or targets are being exceeded?
- *Moving on (what progress means)* – Manage to feed the success and value back into the system. Do not assume it will and do not leave this to someone else or to a later plan.

Conclusions

Planning is a continuous process and plans are the tools we use to ensure that the best processes are applied. Plans are a record of a recent situation and of where we are aiming to be in a specified period of time. They are working tools that help us chart the route we intend to take and the method we intend to use to get there. They are a way of ensuring that everyone involved understands what is going on, what is intended and who is expected to take part.

Plans avoid being over-complicated by breaking things down into manageable parts and by sharing out the responsibility for getting things done across a range of players.

Because plans are working documents the things we learn as we try to carry out the plans will affect the final outcome and shape of what we do. It is unlikely that we will change our objectives or aims for a completely different outcome but what we learn might affect how we get there or how well we do. So, flexibility should be part of the plan and contingencies should be expected and planned for.

When planning to meet your customer needs this element of flexibility is extremely important. Customers change as the external environment changes, their needs change and competitors introduce new factors into the equation. You cannot know everything or be able to predict the future so you must expect things to change and plan ways of responding to change into your plans. This is why listening is so important when dealing with customers and why measurement and monitoring needs to be carried out. It is also why building virtuous cycles into your systems will help.

Competence self-assessment

1 What are audits used for in plans and why should you always try to collect internal *and* external information for your audit?
2 What do the letters in SWOT stand for and which are internal and which are external?
3 What do you have to be careful with when using the SWOT analysis?
4 What are the four quadrants in a 'big picture' box and how can they be used?
5 Describe two methods designed to help you prioritize your activities or objectives.
6 Name and explain the four quadrants in the cost/priority box.
7 Where do you find the areas of balance or compromise in the priority and value boxes? How can you use them?
8 How can you use the ease/value box to help you prioritize your activities or objectives?
9 Name and explain four things that help you make plans work.

Not the end, this is just the start!

If you practise what we preach you will know that no one can sit on their laurels! If you listen to your customers you will hear them ask for new things, better service, improved quality, better care, and so on. If you plan to meet customers' needs effectively you should always be striving to keep ahead of your customers' demands and in front of competitors, too.

This is a book that practises what it preaches. The model for this book took the form of a cycle – a virtuous cycle – with the view that the reader would regularly revisit the processes in this book with the intention of improving and developing the relationships they have identified and begun to nurture with their customers.

We said at the beginning of the book that you would need to develop your listening skills in order to meet your customers' needs fully. Once developed, these skills will cause you to continue the process throughout your working life. Few things remain the same over time and as your products/services change, your customers will also change and their needs will be different. What you learned from your customers last year will be applied this year as you continue to listen and plan for the future. Some periods will be defined by the speed of change and others by consolidation and slower rates of change. But your own circumstances will develop and change, too. So as you move on you will pass on knowledge of familiar markets as you move on to new ones.

Expect technology to change. The pattern of technology-based change has been one of greater involvement for customers, increased interaction between providers and customers, higher levels and broader ranges of information and much greater opportunities and choice from a larger market place.

Along with these changes we will find the same challenges we presented in this book. We will be forced to properly encounter our customers and learn what they want and think – the customers will demand that of us and competition will ensure that we have to respond. There will be greater opportunities to develop and work with customers to improve the effectiveness and efficiency of our delivery but while the responsibility for developing and evaluating the products or services will be more evenly shared between suppliers and customers, it will be the supplier's responsibility to ensure quality and delivery.

The tools and concepts you have worked with here will help you develop your response to this more customer-focused world where competition could just as easily come from across the road as it will from across the world. The systems will make distances appear immaterial or transparent but it will be up to you to ensure that your customers' experiences meet their expectations.

Hence, we have made the assertion that this is only the beginning. No core set of management skills can be assumed to be static and no management practice can be left unevaluated or assumed to be perfect. The good news is that the process is both rewarding and enjoyable. It is just as important for you to enjoy your work as it is for the customer to enjoy the outcome of your efforts. The management process cannot work as a true virtuous cycle if it ignores the well-being and rewarding of those working in it.

Finally, the title of this book warns us that meeting our customers' needs is a continuous process, so how do we know if we are getting anywhere? Do we just assume it is a treadmill we can never get off? Dialogue, exchange, reviews and continuous improvement all ensure that we know where we are as well as where we are going. The final judges of our success are not just our bosses and neither is it our customers. The process we involve ourselves in develops into a method of self-examination as well as a customer-focused approach and as we get better at it we teach ourselves what success is like and hone our skills to achieve more of it. You will end up wanting to exceed not just your customers' expectations but also your own. And that is when things really start to get interesting!

Index